Toward
the
Goal

For Mom and Dad—

For the orange slices, clean jerseys, bug repellent, registration fees, practice transportation, and encouragement during my own days in goal. Thank you for introducing me to the beautiful game—and most of all for your unwavering support through all the game of life.

JVJ

Toward the Goal

The Kaká Story

Jeremy V. Jones &
Janna Jones

ZONDERVAN.com/
AUTHORTRACKER
follow your favorite authors

ZONDERKIDZ

Toward the Goal: The Kaká Story
Copyright © 2010 by Jeremy V. Jones and Janna Jones

This title is also available as a Zondervan ebook.
Visit www.zondervan.com/ebooks.

Requests for information should be addressed to:

Zondervan, *Grand Rapids, Michigan 49530*

Library of Congress Cataloging-in-Publication Data

Jones, Jeremy V.
    Toward the goal : the Kaká story / by Jeremy V. Jones and Janna Jones.
      p. cm. — (Zonderkidz biography)
    ISBN 978-0-310-72003-4 (softcover)
    1. Kaká, 1982- 2. Soccer players—Brazil—Biography. I. Jones, Janna. II. Title.
III. Series.
GV942.7. K35J66 2010
796.334092—dc22   2010001892

Cover design: Kris Nelson
Cover photography: Jeff Mitchell - FIFA/Getty Images
Interior photography: © iStockphoto.com/Zentilia
Interior design and composition: Beth Shagene, Greg Johnson/Textbook Perfect,
and Carlos Eluterio Estrada

Printed in the United States of America

---

10 11 12 13 14 15 /DCI/ 23 22 21 20 19 18 17 16 15 14 13 12 11 10 9 8 7 6 5 4

Contents

A Champion among Champions

It was the biggest game of the year. The winner would be the champion of all of Europe's mighty professional leagues and teams. Soccer clubs across the continent had played each other all season long in the ongoing UEFA Champions League tournament. Now, on May 23, 2007, in approximately ninety minutes of soccer, Italy's A.C. Milan or England's Liverpool would be crowned the best of the best.

Police in riot gear ringed the outside of Olympic Stadium in Athens, Greece. At one point fans without tickets tried to break down a closed gate to storm their way, and the police fired tear gas to repel them.

But the true battle was taking place on the brilliant green grass rectangle at the center of the stadium. Seventy thousand cheering, chanting fans watched as the action unfolded in red and white before them. Milan wore white; Liverpool red.

Liverpool took control of the action early, and the Reds' Jermaine Pennant got the first shot on goal eight minutes in. But Milan's goalkeeper, Dida, made the diving save.

Once Milan settled down the game was evenly matched, and neither side could break through the other's tough defense. It seemed as if the two coaches had prepared their teams so well that the defenses could anticipate every attack.

The Milan team was filled with veteran World Cup winners and European Champions such as Paolo Maldini and Clarence Seedorf, but its superstar was young number twenty-two: Kaká. It was his heroic play in the semifinal game that had secured the victory over Manchester United and propelled the *Rossoneri* (Milan's nickname, referring to their red and black uniforms) to this final game.

Liverpool was well aware of the threat Kaká posed, and used its defensive midfielder Javier Mascherano to dog Milan's most creative playmaker and pressure him constantly. The tactic seemed to work. Kaká and his whole team mustered only one shot on goal during the first half, and it was easily saved by Liverpool's keeper Pepe Reina.

A minute before halftime, Kaká was fouled just outside of Liverpool's penalty area, giving a free kick to Milan. Their free kick specialist Andrea Pirlo placed the silver and blue-starred game ball on the turf twenty-three yards from the goal in the center of the field. Ten yards back, Liverpool lined up eight men in a wall to create a barrier. Anticipation grew as the fans knew that set plays like this were always dangerous opportunities for a team to score a goal. Would this one put Milan ahead at halftime? Would the Milan shooter go straight for the goal, looking for a way around Liverpool's wall? Or would he pass to a teammate who could take a quick shot from another angle?

Milan's striker Filippo Inzaghi had lined up on the edge of Liverpool's wall. As soon as Pirlo struck the ball, he turned and sprinted toward the goal. The shot bent around the inside edge of the wall, curling toward the left side of the goal. Goalkeeper Reina dove to his left and looked like he would cover the shot. But as Inzaghi turned to look back, the ball struck him on the shoulder and deflected back toward the other side of the goal, behind Reina. Goal Milan!

The goal gave Milan momentum that they carried into the second half, pressing their attack as Liverpool's defense began to weaken. The score remained 1–0, however, until the final ten minutes.

In an effort to come from behind as the end of the game approached, Liverpool substituted in another attacker to try to come up with an equalizing goal. Liverpool's Mascherano went out, and Kaká quickly made the most of the opportunity. Shaking Mascherano's shadow, Kaká quickly found some freedom and space on the field. Right away he chipped a pass to Inzaghi in front of the open goal, but the striker couldn't get the shot on goal.

A few minutes later, Kaká received a pass and dribbled the ball with lots of open space toward Liverpool's goal box, shuffled subtly as if he might shoot, then sent a crisp through-ball between three defenders. Inzaghi rushed through from across the center and had only the goalie between him and the net. With one touch he pushed the ball toward the baseline to avoid the charging Reina. Then, from a difficult angle, he sent the ball rolling beneath the goalie's dive, across the goal mouth, and into the opposite side net. Goal!

Inzaghi ran to the corner and grabbed the corner flag. He fell to his knees pumping his fists and shouting, then lowered his face to the ground. Kaká was the first teammate to run and embrace him. Milan had a 2–0 lead.

Liverpool attacked desperately and received a corner kick in the eighty-ninth minute. The ball sailed in to the near corner of the goal box. It was headed across the goal toward Dirk Kuyt near the far post, and Kuyt headed the ball into the back of the net to cut the lead in half.

Two years ago these very same teams had faced off in the 2005 Champions League final. A.C. Milan took a 3–0 lead into halftime, only to see Liverpool unbelievably fight back to send the game into a shootout tiebreaker, then win on penalty kicks. Could the Reds find another miracle comeback?

But time was on Milan's side in this game, and the referee blew his final whistle three minutes later. The Rossoneri were the champions of Europe and arguably of the whole world.

The Italian fans went wild, and Liverpool fans cried.

Kaká and his teammates celebrated joyously, and fans cheered and sang in the stands as confetti rained onto the field. Kaká stripped off his jersey to reveal a white T-shirt with big black lettering that said "I belong to Jesus" in English. The Brazilian star ran a victory lap around the field cheering and waving

Kaká celebrates after beating Liverpool 2–1 to win the Champions League Final soccer match, May 23, 2007.

both arms to the fans as a cluster of cameramen and photographers tried to keep up. Finally, Milan was presented with the huge silver cup.

The victory completed an amazing year for Kaká, but there were even more accolades to come. Many sports magazines had been calling Kaká the best player in the world. In October he was officially named the Federation Internationale des Associations de Footballers Professionels (FIFPro) 2007 World Player of the Year, voted on by more than forty-five thousand soccer professionals around the world.

In December he received the prestigious Ballon d'Or, or Golden Ball, for the best player in world by France Football magazine. And later that month, Kaká was voted the FIFA World Player of the Year by the world's national team coaches and captains.

"It's really special for me — it was a dream for me just to play for São Paulo and one game for Brazil," Kaká said when he accepted the golden trophy. "But the Bible says God can give you more than you even ask for and that is what has happened in my life."

Kaká had been dreaming big since he was a boy, and his faith had carried him even when the odds seemed long that he would ever become a soccer player. But with hard work, determination, and humility he had reached great heights. This is the story of how it all happened.

A Boy in Brazil

Ricardo Izecson dos Santos Leite was known as Ricardinho, which means "Little Richard," for the earliest years of his life. But when his younger brother, Digão, began learning to speak, he couldn't pronounce his brother's name. Kaká (pronounced *ka-KA*) was the best he could do, and the name stuck.

The boys were both born in Brasilia, the capital of Brazil. The city had only been built in 1960, when President Juscelino Kubitschek ordered the capital to be moved from the Atlantic coast to the country's interior savanna region. The nation's constitution had called for the capital to be moved closer to the nation's center as early as 1891. But the world-famous city Rio de Janeiro had remained the seat of the government. City planners laid out Brasilia carefully, and from high up in the sky the center of the metropolis looks like an airplane or a bird.

Kaká and Digão knew the place simply as home. Their father, Bosca Izecson Pereira Leite, was a civil engineer, and their mother, Simone Cristina Santos Leite, a teacher. Both parents loved them very much and took good care of their sons.

Mr. Leite's job brought a move to Cuiabá, a city about six hundred miles west of Brasilia, when Kaká was four. The family moved to São Paulo when Kaká was seven years old, and this city became their permanent home.

Kaká began attending school at the Colegio Baptista Brasileiro, or Brazilian Baptist School. He was a calm, shy kid in school. He was an excellent student who earned good grades, and his teachers hoped that he might grow up one day to be a doctor or engineer.

Like most boys his age, he also enjoyed sports. For a while tennis was his favorite, and he dreamed of winning professional tennis tournaments one day. That was before he got serious about soccer, or *futebol* as it's called in Brazil.

Kaká's first memory of soccer is of going with his father to watch São Paulo play when he was eight. At school he began playing *futsal*, a Brazilian version of indoor soccer played with a smaller ball. That same year a P.E. teacher named Enio told Mr. and Mrs. Leite that they should enroll their son in a special soccer academy. They took his advice and signed Kaká up for a soccer club. In a Brazilian TV story years later, Enio remembered him being better at handling a soccer ball than most of the kids, but still being patient with those who weren't as talented as he was.

Mr. Leite also paid for a membership to train at the São Paulo Football Club's facilities. Like teams in Europe, professional soccer teams in Brazil have their own academies. They even have

Kaká started playing soccer at a young age. Here he plays with a ball in his house in Brazil.

youth teams so they can coach and develop children's soccer talents. As competition gets tougher as age groups rise, the clubs watch for special talent and hope to find their future professional players.

Founded in 1935, São Paulo FC had a long, rich history. It is the most successful club in Brazil, according to the number of championship titles they've received, and is considered the third most popular club behind Flamengo and Corinthians.

The club takes its name from the city where it's located. São Paulo is Brazil's largest metropolis. In fact, it has one of the largest populations in the entire world, with about 20 million people in its metropolitan area. The differences between São Paulo and Rio de Janeiro have been compared to the rivalry between American cities Los Angeles and New York City. Like Los Angeles,

Rio is set in a beautiful coastal and natural setting; it is famous for its flamboyant *Carnaval* celebrations, big glitzy parties, and parades. São Paulo is more like New York, and is known for its art, culture, and sophistication. It is often described as having a European flavor.

Brazil itself is the fifth-largest nation in the world, with nearly 200 million people. Like many South American countries there is a great deal of poverty. Living conditions for working class citizens are considered impoverished by Western standards. Most people fall into either the poor or wealthy classes, with a very small middle class in between.

São Paulo is a wealthier city in general, and São Paulo F.C. was traditionally known as the team of the upper classes. By comparison, Corinthians was founded by members of São Paulo's working class and has maintained strong support from that sector of the population.

Kaká's family was financially comfortable because both of his parents were well-educated professionals. They were able to pay for Kaká's soccer academy tuition and provide him with good opportunities to sharpen his skills, but he would still have to prove himself on the field if he wanted to progress.

At the time, Kaká was unaware of the social structures around him. He was simply a young boy playing a fun game.

One Name Wonders

Kaká, Ronaldo, Pelé, Ronaldinho, Dida, Lucio, Fred … the list of Brazilian players who go by only one name goes on and on. So what's with the one name? It's not only a tradition of Brazilian soccer players; many people in Brazil go by only one name. It's so common that some phone books in Brazil even list them that way rather than by their full names. The one name can be the person's first name, last name, a contraction of the two, or a completely unrelated nickname. Referring to someone by their first name or nickname is a sign of close friendship. In Brazil, calling someone by his nickname shows both care and respect for the person.

There is no definitive answer for where the tradition began. Some say it could have roots in a high illiteracy rate—people went by one shorter name to avoid spelling and writing the full name. Others say the tradition may date back to the time of slavery, when slaves were often recorded and called by only one name. What's certain is that the tradition today is all about personality and individuality. And Brazil's fans love the closeness they feel with players they call by one name.

While Brazil is best known for the tradition, other countries with a large number of one-name players include Portugal, Spain, and Angola.

Brazil

Brazil, or *Brasil* as it's spelled in Portuguese, is the largest country in South America, covering nearly half of the continent and bordering all South American countries except Chile and Ecuador. Its neighbors to the north are Venezuela,

Guyana, Suriname, and French Guiana. It's bordered to the northeast, east and southeast by the Atlantic Ocean. To the south is Uruguay, and to the southwest are Argentina and Paraguay. It borders Bolivia and Peru on the west, and Columbia to the northwest. It's the fifth-largest country in the world after Russia, Canada, China, and the United States (when Hawaii, Alaska, and the territories are included.)

Prior to the arrival of European explorers, the area that is now Brazil was populated by indigenous groups. Explorers from Portugal arrived in the 1500s and named their new land Brazil after the "pau-brasil" wood from which they made red dye. Brazil was settled by the Portuguese and remains the only Portuguese-speaking country in South America as a result of its colonial history.

The majority of Brazil's 190 million people live in Brazil's capital city of Brasília or in its largest cities, São Paulo and Rio de Janeiro. São Paulo is the world's second-most populous city with a population of over 20 million people. But while most of the population is concentrated near the coast, the land of Brazil is incredibly diverse. Brazil is framed by two of the world's largest river systems: the Amazon in the north, and the Paraná River in the south. It has the world's largest rain forest but also includes savannah, wetlands, highlands, and the coastal areas.

And Brazil is rich with natural resources. It has the world's largest reserves of fresh water, tropical forest, and biodiversity. In fact, enough water flows out of the Amazon each day to keep New York City supplied for 10 years! Historically much of the land has been exploited, but there have been increased efforts in recent years to preserve and utilize the country's natural resources. While the country still struggles with high crime in areas and unequal distribution of wealth, it is progressing as a nation. By utilizing its vast natural resources and a large labor pool, it has become a regional economic power and leader in South America.

Jogo Bonito

Almost every young boy in Brazil dreams of becoming a soccer pro at one time or another. Millions devote themselves to pursuing that dream, playing soccer in streets, fields, beaches, empty lots, jungle clearings, or any area large and flat enough. Many Brazilian fathers give their sons soccer balls in their baby cribs, and most Brazilian children know how to juggle a ball by the time they are three years old.

Poor kids often play barefoot and may not even have a real ball. Instead, they might use a bundle of rags, a sock stuffed with newspapers, or any other round object or ball. Besides being a fun sport they love, soccer allows them to dream of making a better life for themselves.

If a child is good enough, he might be spotted by a local scout in the daily street games and given a tryout with a club team. Or like Kaká, he might be spotted in school and recommended to a club. Or he may simply go to a regional tryout held by a club looking for talented players. As Brazil's cities have grown bigger, more modern, and more crowded, an indoor version of the game called *futsal* has become popular and allowed kids to sharpen their skills in gyms or indoor arenas. Private soccer academies have also grown more popular in Brazil, offering kids a way to devote themselves to and become better at the game.

There are many levels of amateur and professional teams across Brazil. The top league is the prestigious Brasileirão Serie A. Its twenty teams have national followings and long histories. Its players are regional and national heroes. The best of the best usually go on to play in Europe, home to the world's richest and most powerful leagues. Many European teams have scouts in Brazil watching for talented kids, and those clubs bring young players overseas to live and train in their own developmental academies.

Whatever the route, the more promise a player shows, the faster and farther he can rise through club ranks and ultimately reach the pros. After all, many Brazilians have gone from childhood poverty to world-superstar status because of their amazing soccer skills. Ronaldo and Ronaldinho are two recent examples of players who rose from Brazilian *favelas*, or slums, to earn million-dollar soccer salaries in Europe, win World Player of the Year awards, and lead the Brazilian national team to World Cup victory.

But beyond the huge salaries of pro players, Brazilian

futebol ignites a passion in its fans and players. Soccer is the national sport, and it is a big part of Brazil's national identity. Brazil has won more World Cup championships than any other nation and shaped the game with its unique style.

There's a common saying about soccer: "England invented it. The Brazilians perfected it." The modern game of soccer was created in England in the 1830s, and it was a Scotsman who brought it to Brazil. A young man named Charles Miller brought two soccer balls home to Scotland with him after he completed his education in England. His father, like many British workers, moved to Brazil to work on the railroads, and Charles went with him. Charles began organizing soccer kickabouts in São Paulo that quickly caught on with the local people. Another Anglo-Brazilian, Oscar Cox, returned from school in Europe and brought the game to Rio de Janeiro. By 1900 the first soccer club was formed, and others followed soon after.

Slavery had only been ended in Brazil in 1888, so there was still much racism and social change taking place there at the turn of the century. The early soccer matches were originally reserved for British and European players of the upper class, but even the poor people noticed. The game was easy to copy—all that was required was a ball. So the former slaves and native Brazilians began playing their own games. They were first allowed to play at the top level when, in 1904, the Bangu Athletic Club in Rio club decided to chose its players regardless of race. The more non-white players became incorporated into the clubs, the more Brazilian the game became.

The British version of the game was formal and regimented. But as Brazilians learned to play the game apart from the European-oriented clubs, they developed their own style that relied more on individual skill and movement.

A match in 1914 that pitted Exeter City from England against a team of Rio and São Paulo's finest players is considered the first Brazilian national team. Brazil won 2–0, and the people found a strong sense of national pride in the team.

That sense of pride and identity grew as Brazil evolved the sport. Brazil won its first World Cup in 1958, then followed with World Cup championships in 1962 and 1970. No other country had reached that mark in World Cup dominance, and the world hadn't yet seen the game played with the creative flair of Brazil and its standout star Pelé.

Pelé's fluid dribbling and ability to control the ball in ways that seemed impossible cemented his legacy as the greatest player ever. He was Brazil's ambassador to the world, and he was soccer's biggest ambassador, spreading the joy and development of the game around the globe, including to the United States when he finished his pro career there in the 1970s.

One aspect that sets soccer apart from other sports is its non-stopping clock. American football resets after each play. Basketball is filled with timeouts, and baseball pauses to switch offense and defense each inning. But soccer runs in one continuous flow with only a halftime break. The result is that every pass, touch, or possession of the ball has the ability to cause a ripple effect on the game as it keeps unfolding. It also gives soccer the ability to surge and flow like a symphony as teams battle to control the conductor's baton of momentum.

It's that graceful flow that has made soccer known as the beautiful game, and it was Pelé who epitomized Brazilian soccer and popularized the sport as *jogo bonito*, the beautiful game. Brazil plays with style and rhythm, flowing with quick unexpected passes, skillful dribbling and dodging, and graceful elegance while attacking the goal.

One nickname of the national team is the Samba Boys. The samba is the upbeat rhythmic music and dance played throughout Brazil. The Brazilians have made soccer look like a graceful dance set to its beat and a joyous celebration to be swept up in.

Soccer was as much a part of the culture Kaká grew up in as the Portuguese language he speaks. It is part of his heritage that shaped him as a player and a person.

Pelé: The Greatest Ever

Born Edson Arantes do Nascimento, Pelé is considered the greatest soccer player of all time. His humble beginnings did not limit his ability, and he went from playing in the streets of Brazil with a "ball" made from a sock stuffed with newspapers to his first World Cup appearance in 1958 at the age of 17. During that World Cup he scored a hat trick (three goals) in the semifinal as well as two goals in the final, leading Brazil to its first World Cup Championship. He is the only player ever to win three World Cup trophies. Pelé spent most of his years playing for the São Paulo team, Santos, and became a national treasure in Brazil.

Pelé is known for his seemingly limitless and varied skills. He was not just an excellent attacker and scorer, he could do it all—dribbling, passing, and seeing the field in a way that few other players could. He was loved in Brazil and around the world.

He retired from club ball in 1971 but later came out of retirement to join the New York Cosmos. His style of play and love of the game gave soccer new life in the United Sates. His influence helped bring the World Cup to the United States in 1994 and played a role in the creation of Major League Soccer (MLS) in 1995.

Along with his spectacular performance as a player, Pelé served as Brazil's minister of sports and became a goodwill ambassador for UNICEF. In 1999 the Olympic Committee voted him Athlete of the Century.

God and Soccer

Kaká's twelfth year was an important one for both his spiritual and soccer life, and the decisions he made then would guide him throughout the rest of his life.

Most Brazilians follow the Catholic tradition of faith and worship, but there have been many new Protestant churches growing in the country in the past few decades. Both of Kaká's parents are evangelical Christians. Their faith guided their home and family, and Kaká grew up with a great respect for faith in God.

"Little by little, I stopped simply hearing people talk about the Jesus my parents taught me. There came a time when I wanted to live my own experiences with God," he said when he was grown up.[1]

When he was twelve he decided to be baptized. It was a meaningful experience that brought him closer to Jesus.

"When I was baptized in 1994, something super-natural happened to me," Kaká later told the British newspaper *Mail on Sunday*.[2] "I cannot explain it, but after that experience I got closer to God; more in tune with him. At that moment I was really born spiritually. I began to know God more in-depth."

The young Christian also became more serious about his future in soccer that same year. He decided he wanted to become a professional and hoped to one day reach the top team at São Paulo FC. "If it doesn't work out as a player, I would certainly go into physical education," he would later tell *The Irish Times*.[3]

His ball-handling abilities and keen knowledge of the game were his best skills and helped him to do well. But his small size kept him from standing out. He just wasn't strong enough physically. When he was twelve, he was the size of a ten-year-old because his bones weren't developing at a normal rate. He continued to lag behind his peers in growth. Kaká was used to being smaller, but it gave him opportunities to learn.

"It was hard, but I learned from it," Kaká later told the soccer magazine *442*. "I learned to fight for what I wanted and that was important."[4]

Life was good at the São Paulo academy. Several hundred boys lived in the dorms there and shared Kaká's dreams. Many, like Marcelo Saragosa, had traveled from far away to pursue their soccer dreams. Marcelo was from the southern Brazilian state Santa Catarina. When he was twelve, his coach invited him to São Paulo for a tryout with the club. Of the two hundred other boys at the tryout, only Marcelo was chosen to stay.

The boys lived at the academy at dormitories similar

to American college dorms. They did their schoolwork there and spent the rest of the time practicing soccer and training. Their favorite practices were the scrimmage games they played against each other. Kaká was known as a disciplined and hard-working student and player. He often woke up two hours early to study so he could maintain his training and practice schedule.

On weekends most of the players would go home with their families. Marcelo's home was too far away, so one week Kaká asked, "Marcelo, do you want to spend Saturday and Sunday with me at my house?"

"Yeah, that would be great," Marcelo answered.

Soon Marcelo was spending

Kaká poses for a picture with a Sao Paulo FC jersey, the club where he played from his childhood until his transfer to AC Milan, in 2003.

every weekend with Kaká and his family in their comfortable São Paulo home. Kaká and Marcelo became best friends, and Marcelo grew to be another son and brother to the family. Mr. and Mrs. Leite would introduce him as "their other son from South Brazil," and kept Marcelo in line along with their own sons.

Marcelo attended church with the Leite family, and Kaká often prayed for Marcelo. Marcelo did not have a relationship with Jesus, but he would see Kaká reading his Bible often. The two friends talked about God and Kaká helped his friend begin a relationship with Jesus.

"He showed me some things that I need to change," Marcelo said. "He helped a lot with the Bible, too."

The boys got involved in a Bible study through *Atletas de Cristo*, or Athletes for Christ, at the academy and learned more about God. It was an important time for them as they grew stronger in their faith.

"It makes me happy to read the Bible every day, to study it and to be in fellowship with God, and learn more and more about Jesus," Kaká would say as an adult. But he was gaining his love for God and his Word even at a young age.[5]

They also had lots of fun, too. One favorite activity of Kaká, Marcelo, and Digão was PlayStation. Of course, their favorite video game was soccer. Kaká and Digão would battle and battle with their digital teams. The boys also played during free time at the club. Kaká always chose AC Milan as his digital team, a foreshadowing of things to come.

São Paulo Futebol Clube

São Paulo FC is the youngest of the major teams from the city and state of São Paulo, but it was still founded in 1930. The Tricolor struggled for a long time to earn themselves a place alongside the state's two traditional giants, Corinthians and Palmeiras.

But the club's motto "Football is an art; we have another approach to the game" helped them build a fan base. So did Artur Friedenreich, the team's legendary goal scorer who netted an incredible 1,329 goals in a twenty-six-year career. Friedenreich was the hero of the crowds packed into São Paulo stadium, known more commonly as Morumbi stadium. Officially, the arena holds 80,500 fans.

Brazil's Diverse People

The people of Brazil are known for their consistently warm, friendly, expressive nature, and yet they are richly diverse and varied in ethnicity and culture. The Portuguese settlers who came during the colonization of Brazil were unlike settlers in many European colonies. Less concerned with conquest of a new land, many were convicts accused of crimes against religion or morality. The majority of them were men, and the resulting lack of Portuguese women meant that relationships and marriage with native Indian women (and later with female African slaves) were more common and accepted than in many other European colonies. During its history of slavery, around four million African slaves were transported to Brazil. That is seven times the number brought to the United States. This resulted in a very large black population—the largest outside of Africa. In fact, only Nigeria has a larger black population than Brazil.

Brazil's history of immigration continued with large numbers of immigrants continuing to come from Portugal, but many also coming from other nations including Germany, Italy, Japan, and the Middle East. The intense and widespread mixing of all these groups has formed a diverse population in Brazil. Almost all Brazilians have some combination of European, African, Native American, Asian, and Middle Eastern lineage. This variety of cultural backgrounds and traditions has brought some conflict to Brazil, but has also added color and flavor to the current culture.

Portuguese remains the dominant language of Brazil, but this mixing of peoples and cultures has influenced the language as well. The Indian and African dialects found throughout Brazil have impacted the development of Portuguese not only in Brazil, but around the world. As for religion, the Roman Catholic influence of Portugal has remained dominant, as roughly seventy-five percent of today's Brazilians belong to the Roman Catholic Church.

The Accident

Kaká signed his first professional contract when he was fifteen. São Paulo welcomed him to its youth team, which is the same age range as Under–17 in the United States.

That year Kaká was five feet, three inches tall and weighed 110 pounds—still much smaller than the other players. The officials at São Paulo FC took him to see doctors in the city to see if they could stimulate his bone development. The doctors put Kaká on a special diet high in carbohydrates and creatine, a natural amino acid used to promote muscle growth.

Kaká's body began to respond, and he checked in with the doctors every three months. By the time he was seventeen he had reached five feet, nine inches but was still skinny. "I used to reassure his parents by saying, 'Don't worry, he'll grow. The rest of you are all tall,'" remembered Turibio Leite de Barros Neto, São Paulo's physical trainer.[1]

Trainers continued to help him, and Kaká worked hard on a muscle building plan. In another year and a half he had added another twenty-two pounds to his frame, much of it muscle.

The teenager also had to deal with myopia, or near-sightedness. That meant he could see objects that were close, but people or objects far away were blurry. In decades past, it had been a national scandal when someone started a rumor that Pelé was nearsighted. But medical technology had advanced since then, and Kaká simply wore contact lenses to give him clear vision down the entire length of the soccer field. Later, as an adult, he had surgery to give him perfect vision permanently.

Kaká moved up to São Paulo's junior team, the equivalent of U–20 in the United States. His new size definitely helped him on the field to be able to out-muscle other players for the ball. However, he wasn't one of the eleven starting players and didn't get much opportunity to play in games for the juniors.

But the young midfielder took advantage of every opportunity to learn and grow as a player. He loved it when the junior team got to scrimmage against the pro team. And he had little patience for players who would dive, or take a fall on purpose, to try to get the referee to call a foul or award a penalty kick in their favor. He learned from every coach he had.

"The ones that didn't like me taught me perseverance, patience, how to fight for what I wanted," Kaká told *442* later in life. "From the ones that did pick me I learned about technique and tactics." [2]

Overall Kaká's career was moving in the right direction, but it almost came to end when he was eighteen in October 2000.

In the middle of the Paulista Junior Championship, Kaká received two yellow cards, so he was suspended from the following game. He took advantage of the break to visit his grandparents in Caldas Novas, a popular tourist area in central Brazil known for its hot water springs. While there he went to a water park. Kaká slid down one particular water slide headfirst, but at the end his head struck the bottom of the pool and snapped his neck. It hurt, and his head was bleeding. He needed four stitches, and doctors took an x-ray. But everything seemed normal.

Kaká went home to São Paulo and practiced for two days, but the pain in his neck was unbearable. Doctors took more x-rays, which revealed a frightening diagnosis. Kaká had broken his neck. More precisely, he had fractured the sixth vertebrae in the top of his spine. Doctors told the Leite family that their son was lucky not to be paralyzed and lucky to even be walking normally.

Back home the family thanked God for protecting Kaká. They began praying for healing and asking friends to pray as well. Kaká had to wear a neck brace and lay in bed for two months. But at the end of that time, he was completely healed.

"[The doctors] were talking about luck, and my family

was talking about God," Kaká later told *The Independent*. "We knew that it was his hand that had saved me."[3]

The accident was a key point in Kaká's life, and one that shaped him permanently. Spiritually, it confirmed his faith and taught him that God was taking care of him. It was a difficult time that prompted Kaká to pray much more and trust God more deeply. Looking back on the event later in life, Kaká told Athletes in Action, "I do not think that it was a coincidence. I believe God had a purpose in that accident."[4]

The recovery period also gave him a lot of time to think. Would he be able to play soccer again? If he did, what did he want his future to look like? What did he want to accomplish in life? As the athlete waited and considered what might happen, he made a list of ten goals:

1. Return to soccer
2. Become a professional
3. Become first string (one of the top twenty-five players)
4. Fight for a position in the top eighteen
5. Win a starting spot
6. Compete in the Under-20 World Cup
7. Be called to the adult national team
8. Play on the adult national team
9. Compete in the World Cup
10. Transfer to a big club in Italy or Germany

He returned to the game he loved, focused on accomplishing his new objectives. No one could have guessed how soon he would need a new list of goals.

More Than One Way to Kick a Ball

Brazil is so obsessed with soccer that it has spilled over into the formation of many related games:

Futsal: Somewhat like a cross between soccer and ice hockey, futsal is incredibly popular in Brazil and around the world. In 2000, 160 countries applied to enter the World Championship. With five players to a side, this game is played on an indoor basketball court with a smaller ball and twenty minute halves.

Button football: Soccer had barely been introduced to Brazil when kids started tearing buttons off their jackets to play a table-top version. They would flick their buttons at a small ball to try to get it into a miniature net. Today the game can be bought as a kit, and official buttons contain the names and faces of popular players.

Beach soccer: With so many Brazilians living near the beach, it is natural that they started playing their favorite sport on the sand. Beach football in Brazil peaked in the 1950s when there was still room on the uncrowded beaches to play. But today's beach soccer is a compact and high-scoring version that is still popular.

Footvolley: A combination of soccer and volleyball, this incredibly popular game is played on a beach volleyball court with two players on each side. The catch? Players can only use their feet, head, and chest.

The Accident

Footbull: Played for fun at rodeos in rural areas of Brazil, spectators are chosen for two teams in the arena. Then a (relatively gentle) bull is released and the crowd is entertained watching the teams go for the ball, and the bull go for the teams.

Instant *Craque*

Kaká's life was about to change dramatically.

Once he was healthy again, he returned to his role on the club: a hard-working reserve midfielder on the junior team who didn't see much playing time in games. One day, the coach of the Tricolor professional team, Vadão, asked the junior's coach for a midfielder and a forward to fill out his roster for a game the next day. The junior's coach pointed out Kaká.

"He doesn't play much because I have my starting eleven right now," the coach said. "But he's a good player."

Coach Vadão took his colleague's word and brought Kaká up to the pro team in early 2001. He played well in his professional game, even scoring a goal to help São Paulo defeat Santos 4–1.

March 7, 2001 was the day that Kaká went from

promising young player to superstar. The game was the final of the Torneio Rio-São Paulo, or Rio-São Paulo Tournament, a yearly contest that determined the champion of the two major city's teams. São Paulo faced the powerful club Botafogo, but the game was held at the Tricolor's home stadium, the Morumbi, in front of 71,000 fans. The atmosphere was especially electric because São Paulo had never won this prestigious tournament.

Things didn't look good for the Tricolor, though, when Donizete of Botafogo scored in the thirty-ninth minute. The Fagão held the lead deep into the second half, and São Paulo's coach knew he needed to make some changes to have a chance at victory. He turned to his bench and brought Kaká into the game in the second half as a substitute for the future national star Luis Fabiano.

With ten minutes left in the game, a Paulista teammate played a high looping pass from midfield toward the right side of Botafogo's penalty box. Another player headed the ball back toward Kaká, who was on the center of the eighteen-yard line. He stuck out his right foot to receive the ball. It flipped behind the back of his defender. Kaká dodged a step to his left and the ball bounced once in front of him. The goalkeeper charged off his line. Kaká powered a shot low along the ground, beneath the diving goalie's outstretched arm and into the goal just inside the post.

"Goooooal, Kaká of São Paulo!" the TV announcer shouted.

Kaká's teammates jumped all over him. Fans danced

in the stands, and fireworks exploded over the Morumbi. São Paulo still had a chance.

Botafogo pressed hard to try to score a winning goal and had some dangerous opportunities. With eight minutes left, the Fagão had a dangerous free kick from the left wing just outside São Paulo's penalty box. Kaká ran across the field waving his arms to urge the crowd to cheer and chant louder. The kick sailed toward the goal but São Paulo's defense headed it away.

But Botafogo controlled the ball and attempted another shot from the eighteen-yard line. Stopped by the Paulista defense! And the counter attack was on. The São Paulo defender passed the ball forward and a midfielder raced with it up the right side of the field. He dribbled toward the middle of the field and sent a perfect curving pass to the left where Kaká came sprinting forward.

Kaká took two touches—left foot, right foot—and was inside Botafogo's penalty box. Three defenders had raced back, and now two were on him. He took a long step left, dragged his right for a split-second, almost hopping forward twice on his left foot. The defender lunged to his right as he faced Kaká. Suddenly Kaká tapped the ball back toward the center and pulled back his right foot to fire a low shot on goal. It rocketed inches above the grass between both defenders, just past the fingertips of the diving goalkeeper, and into the net.

"Goooooooal! For São Paulo!" the TV announcer shouted again. "Kaká! Shirt number thirty-three! His second goal turns the game!"

Teammates buried Kaká under a jumping huddle. Fans embraced in the stands, and the coach pumped both fists in the air. More fireworks lit the night sky overhead.

Eight minutes later the referee blew the final whistle. São Paulo had won! In less than two minutes, Kaká had scored two goals to secure victory and bring the elusive championship to São Paulo.

Kaká raised both hands above his hands and pointed toward the sky. Teammates em-

Kaká in action during the Sao Paulo and Guarani Paulista championship match, March 25, 2001.

braced their new hero. Fans waved sparklers and shot off their own firecrackers in the stands. As the Tricolor celebrated, reporters swarmed around Kaká.

"Kaká, two goals, eighteen years old. It's got to be emotional," a reporter said, thrusting a microphone in Kaká's face.

"It's very emotional," the new hero replied. "God is faithful. I'm not saying that God made the goals, but he gave me the opportunity."

The eighteen-year-old's life would never be the same. He was now a *craque*, the Portuguese word for ace.

São Paulo FC Titles

The São Paulo Football Club is one of the most successful club teams in Brazil, holding the most national league and international titles of any Brazilian club. Their championships include:

FIFA Club World Cup: 2005

Intercontinental Cup: 1992, 1993

Libertadores Cup: 1992, 1993, 2005

Campeonato Brasileiro Série A: 1977, 1986, 1991, 2006, 2007, 2008

Sudden Fame

Overnight everyone knew who Kaká was. Before the Rio-São Paulo tournament, he lived a normal life and could go anywhere without being recognized. Not anymore.

Two weeks after his breakout game, he and Marcelo went to a shopping mall. "Hey, Kaká!" someone shouted. Quickly there were about a hundred people clamoring around and pushing to get close to their new star. "Kaká! Kaká!" they shouted, trying to get autographs and meet him. Kaká and Marcelo couldn't even walk. They had to have help from the security guards to be able to leave.

Interestingly, before the Rio-São Paulo Tournament the team and media had been spelling his name with *c*'s, Caca. The player had asked them before to change it, but nothing had been done. Now that his name was on the whole city's lips, both quickly corrected the spelling to Kaká.

Girls especially loved the young soccer star. After all, he was young and good-looking. The girls formed fan clubs and Web sites and posted pictures of their favorite player. They wanted to know everything about him, especially whether or not he had a girlfriend! They also mailed gifts and wrote letters expressing their admiration and love. Kaká began receiving fifty letters each day. His mother tried to answer them all, but the numbers were simply too much.

The media wanted as much of Kaká as possible too, and his face began to appear on many magazine covers, from sports publications to *Istoe Gente*, Brazil's edition of *People* magazine. It took some getting used to, and Kaká seemed shy at first. But he got plenty of practice and quickly got used to speaking to reporters and the media.

Brazil loves its celebrities, especially its futebol stars, so Kaká and his family weren't completely taken by surprise. What was surprising was how quickly it came. Still, Kaká remained humble and gracious about all the attention and expressed appreciation for his fans' support when he spoke to the press about it. He looked at his new fame and success as a blessing from God and a platform that would allow him to share God's love with many people.

Kaká's family also supported him and helped to deal with all the new attention. He maintained the same lifestyle he always had and didn't let his fame change his attitude or outlook. He always wore a bracelet that read

Jesus, and his trademark celebration became pointing to the sky with both arms upraised to give thanks to God. He also remained loyal to his friends.

One friend and fellow player, Maldonado, told *Istoe Gente* magazine that Kaká hadn't changed, even with all his achievements. "Kaká is a good friend who I can talk to about anything," he said.[1]

One thing Kaká didn't talk about, though, was girls— even to his best friend Marcelo. He was simply too focused on soccer. "In order for me to have a girlfriend, it would have to be a fundamental point in my life," he told *Istoe Gente*. "I can't be thinking of her when I should be concentrating and preoccupied with the game."[2]

He avoided girls who only wanted to get close to him because he was a famous soccer player by not going to dance clubs and wild parties. Instead, he preferred to hang out with his family or friends, and he only dated girls who were already friends or were friends of his friends.

On the field, Kaká's heroic performance against Botafogo had earned him a starting position for São Paulo, and he made the most of it. He scored twelve goals in twenty-seven games during his rookie season.

Sports writers and fans compared him to great Brazilian players, such as Leonardo, Raí, and Socrates. Kaká was honored. Raí had been his favorite player growing up, and Kaká had even followed the São Paulo great into the locker room to ask for an autograph once! But Kaká remained focused on his own game.

"They say I look like Raí and that's a honor. He's an excellent man and a great player," Kaká told *Veja* magazine. "At the beginning everyone searched for references, but that will slowly pass until I make my own mark as Kaká."[3]

Unbelievably, Kaká had achieved the first eight of his ten goals fifteen months after his life-threatening accident that should have ended his career. But the final two were the biggest of all: the World Cup and the European leagues. Some players worked for years and never made the national team or the world's top leagues.

Raí

Kaká often names the Brazilian player Raí as one of his biggest influences. Raí Souza Vieira de Oliveira was born on May 15, 1965. He played club football in Brazil, including for São Paulo from 1987–1993. He then left Brazil and played for Paris St. Germain for five years before returning to São Paulo in 1998 for the end of his career, retiring in 2000.

Raí was a midfielder and, while he didn't make a huge impact on the international soccer scene, he was arguably São Paulo FC's best player of all time, having won every kind of championship for the team during his time there.

"I admired him because he was the top player at São Paulo when I was starting out," says Kaká. "He was a leader who decided games and he was the big name. He was an elegant player and very talented, and that impressed me."[4]

Zico

Another of Kaká's favorite players was Zico, the Brazilian soccer sensation of the time when Kaká was young. Zico is considered one of the best midfielders the world has ever seen. Born Arthur Antunes Coimbra in 1953 in Rio de Janeiro, Brazil, Zico played for the Brazilian national team in the 1978, 1982, and 1986 World Cups. Brazil didn't win any of those championships, even though the 1982 team was one of their strongest national teams ever. He played the bulk of his professional career for the Brazilian club Flamengo, but also spent a few years in Italy and Japan. He also went on to coach in Japan, including the Japanese national team in the 2006 World Cup. On the field, Zico made seemingly impossible goals in all imaginable ways. He was a free kick specialist and playmaking midfielder with excellent vision of the field. As a result, he also dished out many assists.

The Yellow and Green

Kaká caught the eye of more than the Brazilian girls. European scouts took note of this young player and began to consider his potential role on their teams. But perhaps the most important head to turn Kaká's way was that of Luiz Felipe Scolari, the head coach of Brazil's national team.

Coach Scolari called Kaká to train with the *Seleção*, or Selection, as Brazilians call their national team. On January 31, 2002, Kaká pulled on the famous yellow and green jersey of his country for the first time. The match was a friendly against Bolivia. That meant the game didn't count toward any qualification or placement for the World Cup, but both sides wanted to win. It was basically a scrimmage with international pride on the line, and a chance for players like Kaká to gain experience and test their mettle against other nations.

For Kaká it was a momentous occasion. He told his

friend Marcelo that when he put the national jersey on, everything changed. "For a soccer player, there is no more beautiful thing to do," Marcelo recalled later.

Brazil defeated Bolivia 6–0, and Kaká played the second half. He didn't score, but he did make a positive impression on Scolari. The coach called upon him for another match against Iceland in March. This time he started the game and played all ninety minutes. He even scored his first goal for Brazil's national team in the forty-seventh minute to help Brazil claim a decisive 6–1 victory.

On May 23, Kaká went to the São Paulo training center to get treatment for an ankle injury. He told his parents he would be gone all day, but he returned early in the afternoon to surprise his parents. They turned on the TV to watch Coach Scolari announcing the twenty-three players who would be on the roster for the World Cup. There was no surprise about Brazil's national stars such as Ronaldo, Ronaldinho, Rivaldo, and Cafu. But when Coach Scolari announced the twenty-third and final player on the squad, joyous celebration broke out.

Fabrice Coffrini/AFP/Getty Images

Kaká controls the ball during a friendly football game against FC Luzern Selection, in preparation for the 2006 World Cup, May 30, 2006, in Basel, Switzerland.

"Kaká of São Paulo," he told the nation. Kaká was going to the World Cup in South Korea and Japan.

Brazilians were worried about their team heading into the world's greatest soccer competition. Expectations were always sky-high for the Seleção, partly because their team had built such an astonishing record of international dominance. At that point, Brazil had won four World Cup championships, more than any other nation. Even more, in its twelve previous World Cup qualifying campaigns combined, they had only lost one match.

This time the Brazilians had lost six games in reaching the World Cup, and they barely qualified at all. It took a victory over Venezuela in the final match to secure the fourth and final qualifying spot from South America. Even Ecuador placed higher, a team that had never before qualified for a World Cup. The Golden Squad appeared tarnished heading to the world's grandest tournament.

To make matters worse for fans, the previous 1998 World Cup in France had been viewed as a huge disappointment. Brazil had been viewed as a favorite to win. They reached the final game but were destroyed 3–0 by the host team.

Superstar Ronaldo had experienced a mysterious illness before the match, and it became part of the focus of government hearings and investigations into the national soccer federation. Brazil's top levels of soccer organization experienced upheaval and chaos, and the nation demanded more from their Seleção.

"It's a big responsibility to play on the Brazil team because as everyone knows, when it's time for the World

Cup, the players on the team become more important than the president," said defender Edmilson.[1]

"From the moment you become a professional you have to learn to deal with the pressures and the fact that in football, Brazil is always favorite," Ze Roberto added in *The Prize*.[2]

This was the difficult climate Kaká was heading into, but nothing could dampen his elation over being chosen for the team heading to the first World Cup to be hosted in Asia. One bizarre event had helped him make the squad: another talented attacking midfielder named Djalminha who was seen as competition for Kaká's spot on the roster had gotten mad and headbutted Coach Scolari during training. While he admitted the event had influenced his decision, Scolari insisted that Kaká's performance had made the real difference.

Kaká was seen as the baby of the team. He was the younger brother in the Family Scolari, the up-and-comer brought along for experience, just as Ronaldo had been in 1994 and Ronaldinho in 1998. That shared experience helped Kaká and Ronaldinho bond instantly, and Kaká looked to the outgoing superstar to help him learn the ropes of this new level. "Everything that I needed, I asked him—including what type of toothpaste to use," Kaká later told *Istoé Gente*.[3]

Maybe he would pick up some goal-scoring tips from the Brazilian phenomenon as well.

One Team, Many Names

Just as Brazilian players are known by their nicknames, so is its national team. The most common name is *A Seleção* which means "the selection." But seleção is also the Portuguese term used for any team from any country, so it's not unusual for Brazilians to distinguish the national team with the names *Seleção Brasileira* or, more specifically, *A Seleção Brasileira de Futebol*.

The team is also commonly called *O Canarinho*, which means "the little canary." This name has been around since the 1950 World Cup when it was popularized by a cartoonist named Fernando Pierucutti.

Other nicknames for Brazil's team include *Pentacampeões* (Five-time champions), the *Canarinhos* (Canaries), *Verdeamarelos* (Green and Yellows) or the *Auriverdes* (Green and Golds) — the latter three inspired by the national flag and team colors. Other names, such as the Samba Boys or Samba Kings, have come from other news media in other countries.

Brazil's World Cup Leaders

Three players from Brazil have appeared in four World Cup tournaments each. They are led only by Lothar Matthäus of Germany and Antonio Carbajal of Mexico, who have each played in five World Cups. The leading Brazilians are:
Pelé (1958, '62, '66, '70)
Djalma Santos (1954, '58, '62, '66)
Cafu (1994, '98, 2002, '06)

World Champion

Brazil opened the World Cup with a 2–1 victory over Turkey and never looked back. Ronaldo did the same, scoring against Turkey and going on to be the tournament's highest scorer with eight goals overall. Brazilians were relieved to see their beloved hero finding the net.

In the Canarinho's third and final game of the opening round, Brazil held a solid lead over Costa Rica. Coach Scolari turned to his bench and sent Kaká into the game for the final twenty-five minutes. The rookie played well and Brazil won 5–2, securing first place in its group and advancing to the knockout rounds.

Next up for Brazil was Belgium. A controversial call cancelled a Belgian goal that would have given them a 1–0 lead, but Brazil ended up winning 2–0. The quarter-finals brought an always charged Brazil versus England match—the game's inventors against its perfecters.

England claimed the lead in the twenty-third minute on a Michael Owen goal, giving Brits hope that their country could regain soccer supremacy. But at forty-five minutes, Rivaldo equalized just before halftime. Ronaldinho struck quickly in the second half. He sent a screaming free kick that kissed the bottom of the cross-bar and landed in the net as the English's goalkeeper David Seaman watched flatfooted. But Ronaldinho later received a harsh red card that sent him out of the game, and Brazil had to play with only ten men for the game's final thirty-two minutes. They still held on to win and advance.

The semifinal game was a rematch of Brazil's first game against Turkey, and once again the yellow and green prevailed. This time Ronaldo scored his sixth goal of the tournament to deliver a 1–0 victory.

Meanwhile, on the other side of the bracket, Germany relied on a single goal by Michael Ballack and stellar goalkeeping by Oliver Kahn to down two hot under-dogs: the United States in the quarterfinals and hosts Korea Republic in the semis. However, Ballack's second booking with a yellow card against Korea meant that Germany's star would have to sit out of the final.

The table was set for a dual of soccer superpowers: Brazil and Germany on June 30, 2002. Germany was expected to hang back and rely on its defense, but the Germans came out attacking and looking like the more dangerous team in the first half. Brazil still had scoring chances but even Ronaldo couldn't convert them. He blew two golden opportunities in the first half. As the first half wound down, teammate Kleberson struck the German crossbar and goalkeeper Kahn came up with a huge save of a Ronaldo blast. The game remained a scoreless tie at halftime.

Germany kept up the attack again in the second half, and a Jens Jeremies' header was blocked on the goal line by Brazilian defender Edmilson. The Brazilian keeper Marcos was also forced to deflect a thundering thirty-yard German free kick off his post to keep it out of the net. The battle continued.

Then Ronaldo caught fire midway through the second half. Rivaldo fired a shot on goal in the sixty-seventh minute. It appeared that the goalie Kahn should have caught it, but he could only deflect it. Ronaldo pounced on the rebound and sent the ball into the net past the diving Kahn. Twelve minutes later Ronaldo slotted the ball past Kahn again, giving Brazil a 2–0 lead that they would not surrender.

As the game's final minutes ticked away, Coach Scolari told Kaká to warm up on the sidelines. He was going in the game. The twenty-year-old stood on the sideline of the World Cup final, waiting to set foot on the pitch as the referee blew his final whistle. There was never a break in the play to let him in the game. Still, Kaká was a world champion.

The Brazilian sideline erupted into wild celebration. Kaká ran onto the field directly to teammates Edmilson and Lucio. The three immediately fell to their knees, clasped hands, and prayed. "I believe that the emotions ran high, but the important part for us was to kneel and give glory to God," Lucio later said on *The Prize*.[1]

Once they had thanked God, they got up and embraced. The Christian teammates wore white T-shirts with different messages about God. Kaká's read "I belong to Jesus." Edmilson's said "Jesus loves you" and Lucio's "God is faithful." They waved to fans and celebrated with the rest of the team. Kaká draped a Brazilian flag around his shoulders. Many of the players wept with joy.

If playing in the World Cup was another goal accomplished for Kaká, holding the trophy aloft as World Cup champion was a dream come true. Team captain Cafu lifted the golden cup first, and the entire nation of Brazil rejoiced. "It's a fantastic feeling to be a Brazilian tonight," Ronaldo said after the match.[2]

It was many people's favorite moment when the tearful Ronaldo raised the cup, but Kaká will never forget when the superstar striker handed the cup to Kakito, as Ronaldo called him. Back in the locker room, the entire squad joined hands and knelt in a circle to pray and thank God for their victory. All of this was only the beginning of the celebration.

"To get to the World Cup at twenty, to be with the great players, was amazing," Kaká later said to London's *Daily Mail*. "You learn a lot from the players — to create, to keep trying even if you make a mistake, because at some point you will get it right. And you lose a bit of fear. You realize that, although the players are extraordinary, they are normal people."[3]

It was invaluable experience that Kaká hoped to be able to put to good use later.

World Cup Awards

Every team's goal at the World Cup is to win the championship. But there are other honors given out to teams and individual players. These six awards are also presented at the end of the World Cup:

The Golden Ball: Presented to the most outstanding player as decided by a vote of media members. The Silver Ball and the Bronze Ball are also given to the players finishing second and third in the voting.

The Golden Shoe: This award is sometimes called the Golden Boot, and is given to the tournament's top goal scorer. Recently, Silver and Bronze shoe awards have been awarded to the second and third top goal scorers as well.

The Yashin Award: Given to the best goalkeeper, decided by the FIFA Technical Study Group.

The Best Young Player Award: Given to the best player who is 21 years old or younger at the start of the calendar year. This award is also decided by the FIFA Technical Study Group.

The FIFA Fair Play Trophy: The team with the best record of fair play is handed this award. It is decided by a points system and criteria established by the FIFA Fair Play Committee.

The Most Entertaining Team: The general public gets to vote on the team that has been most entertaining for fans.

The World Cup Trophy

Stolen twice, protected from the Nazis, sold at auction, accidentally broken, and recreated—the World Cup trophies have lived an exciting life.

• There have been two official trophies since the World Cup began in 1930. The first was called *Victory,* and later renamed *The Jules Rimet* trophy in honor of the former FIFA president. The second is the FIFA World Cup trophy still in use today.

• The *Victory* trophy was held in Italy during World War II. Fearing the cup would not be safe at the bank in Rome, the Italian Vice President hid it in a shoebox under his bed to keep Nazis from taking it.

• Four months before the 1966 World Cup, the trophy was stolen from an exhibition. It was found wrapped in newspaper at the bottom of a suburban garden hedge in South London by a dog named Pickles.

• In light of security issues, a secret replica was made and used in post-match celebrations. That replica was bought by FIFA at an auction in 1997 for such a high price that some speculate the trophy being sold wasn't the replica, but the genuine cup.

• In line with the original rules, Brazil got to keep the trophy permanently in 1970 with their third World Cup win. But they didn't keep it for long—it was stolen again in 1983 from a display at the Brazilian Football Confederation in Rio de Janeiro. The trophy was never recovered and the investigation concluded it was melted down for its gold. A replacement was commissioned and presented in Brazil in 1984.

• In need of a new cup for 1984, FIFA commissioned artist Silvio Gazzaniga. The new creation was gold with two layers of malachite, a green stone. Unlike the previous trophy, this one is the permanent property of FIFA, and each winning team has its name engraved on the name plate on the bottom of the trophy.

• Italy won the Cup in 2006. Just days after their win, it was reported that a piece of green malachite had broken off and was glued back on.

What will the future hold for the trophy? Stay tuned. It's not easy being the World Cup.

Europe Calling

The Seleção were national heroes. Their 2002 World Cup championship was the nation's fifth. Brazil had now won a World Cup on all five of the continents that had hosted the event.

As their chartered Varig Airlines jet flew home, it was met by military jets to provide an escort for the final few miles. The team jet had its fuselage painted with the players' faces, and it circled over the capital, Brasilia, so the whole city could salute the team.

After landing, Cafu came through the plane's door first and held the World Cup trophy over his head. The city dressed in bright yellow and green went wild. Fireworks exploded. An Air Force band struck up a samba beat, and the party was on.

Next came the parade to the Presidential palace. The players loaded onto two trucks, and it took them four hours to drive the nine miles past several hundred thousand screaming fans.

Brazilians love their futebol team, and they love to celebrate. Life is even better when the two come together.

Expectations were high for Kaká back at São Paulo, and the attacking midfielder continued his winning ways during the 2002 season. He scored ten goals in twenty-two games that year and won the Bola de Ouro, or Golden Ball. The award is given to the best player of the Brazilian League. The Tricolor also came close to winning Brazil's national championship, finishing the regular season in first place but losing in the playoffs. Even though the Paulistas didn't win the championship, Kaká was awarded the tournament's Golden Ball award for the best player.

Much of São Paulo's success was due to Kaká, and São Paulo rewarded him with a $20 million contract. Instead of rushing out to buy a fancy car, Kaká used his money to help pay his brother Digão's college tuition.

Early in 2002, Kaká had met a beautiful girl named Carolina Celico. She had long dark hair and brown eyes. Mr. Leite knew her mother, who was the director of the international fashion design company Dior in Brazil. Their parents introduced them, and Kaká and Caroline exchanged phone numbers.

Kaká went to see Caroline for her fifteenth birthday and began to get to know her. She was younger than the nineteen-year-old Kaká, but that didn't bother him.

His only concern was that she didn't share his Christian faith—yet.

The two began dating after Kaká returned from the World Cup. He took her to church and told her about his relationship with Jesus, and soon she too entrusted her life to Christ. The couple fell in love and began dreaming of marriage. But Caroline was still in school, and they would have to wait several years before that could happen. There would be challenges along the way.

There were also challenges coming for Kaká on the soccer field. Other teams knew that he was São Paulo's leader and playmaker, so they put their best defenders on Kaká to try to shut down the Tricolor attack. Kaká's schedule became extra busy as he also played internationally for the Brazilian Under-23 team. And he also had to deal with an injury, a muscle tear that needed to heal.

Fans continued to mob Kaká in public, and their expectations grew. They wanted a championship, and they wanted it soon. Kaká's goal-scoring dropped off early in the season, and some fans began to boo him on the field. Some criticized him, saying he was too focused on moving to a European team. Several clubs there had expressed interests, and Kaká's agent was negotiating with them and São Paulo FC about money and contractual terms.

Kaká handled all the pressure with his usual grace, saying that it was good preparation for being a player on a national championship-caliber team or one who could make it in the top European leagues.

Manchester United, the world-famous powerhouse from the English Premier League, showed interest in bringing Kaká to its club. German giant Bayer Leverkusen of the Bundesliga offered about 15 million euros, and Brescia of the Italian Serie A offered around 12.5 million. CSKA Moscow in Russia was also interested. But Kaká had his heart on one team, and they were in the

Kaká shows the scarf of his new team, A. C. Milan, as he arrives at the San Siro stadium in Milan, Italy.

running, too. AC Milan had always been his favorite. Plus the former Brazil and São Paulo player Leonardo was an executive with Milan, and he was eager to bring Kaká to Italy.

A deal was reached. In July 2003, Kaká was headed for Italy to be a part of Milan's Rossoneri, or Red-Blacks. He would be paid 8.5 million Euros, about 10.6 million U.S. dollars at the time.

The tenth and final goal from Kaká's list was accomplished in only two and half years. It was time to set his sights on new challenges. Finding challenges wouldn't be any trouble in the excellent Italian league.

The Brazilian Pro League

The highest division of Brazilian football is called Campeonato Brasileirão da Série A. It is often referred to as simply Brasileirão. Twenty teams qualify for this division each year, and Flamengo and São Paulo have dominated competition since this national league began in 1971.

In and Out of the League

Promotion and relegation is a system used by sports leagues worldwide, especially in European football leagues. At the end of each season, teams are transferred between divisions according to their ranking. The best-ranked teams from a lower division are promoted to the next-highest division, while the lowest-ranked teams in a higher division are relegated to the lower division. In Brasileirão, four teams are relegated each year and replaced by four teams being promoted, to make up the new list of twenty.

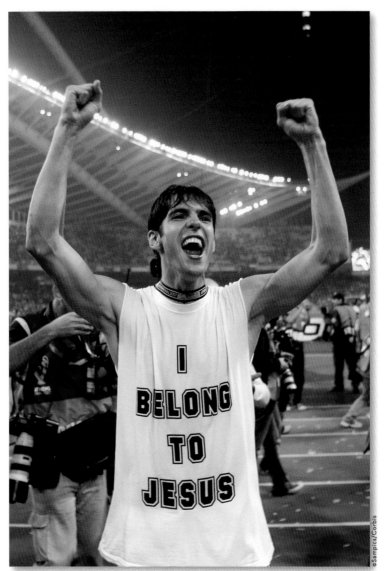

Kaká celebrates after beating Liverpool 2-1 to win the Champions League Final soccer match, May 23, 2007.

Kaká arrives with the Golden Ball in downtown Milan's Duomo square, Dec. 2, 2007. Kaká won the Golden Ball award after helping the Italian club win the Champions League title with some standout performances.

Real Madrid's Kaká kicks the ball during a Spanish La Liga soccer match against Racing Santander at the Santiago Bernabeu stadium, Nov. 21, 2009.

Associated Press/Shizuo Kambayashi

Kaká works out during AC Milan's practice session for the Club World Cup soccer championship in Yokohama, Japan. Kaká always works hard at practice and continues pushing himself to improve his skills.

Kaká kicks the ball during his team's practice session for the Club World Cup soccer championship at Yokohama International Stadium.

Associated Press/Katsumi Kasahara

Kaká shoots during the Champions League soccer match against Zurich at the Santiago Bernabeu stadium in Madrid, Nov. 25, 2009.

Kaká, right, and Heerenveen's Mika Vayrynen, vie for the ball during their UEFA Cup group E soccer match at Abe Lenstra stadium in Heerenveen, The Netherlands, Oct. 23, 2008.

Kaká during an Italian major league soccer match against Lazio in Milan, Italy, Sept. 10, 2006.

Kaká reacts during a press conference after his presentation at the Santiago Bernabeu stadium in Madrid, June 30, 2009. Kaká ushered in Real Madrid's latest "galactico" era as the Spanish club gave him a rock star welcome with an unveiling in front of at least 50,000 fans.

Benvenuti in Italia

Kaká was a bit of a mystery arriving in Italy. When it comes to club teams and national leagues, Europe is the center of the football universe. The biggest players, teams, and leagues exist there—along with the biggest money and power. Because the countries are close together geographically and their teams compete against each other in Union of European Football Associations (UEFA) leagues, many fans know about the players in other countries. Brazil is known and respected worldwide, but the average European soccer fan doesn't necessarily follow Brazil's up and comers—until they head to Europe, that is.

European soccer is generally considered more physical and tactical than South American soccer. South American soccer has a reputation for being more stylistic and free-flowing. It is not uncommon for South

American players to struggle with the adjustment to Europe at first, and Milan's coach Carlo Ancelotti wanted to give his new twenty-one-year-old import time to settle into his new club and continent. He and the team's leaders expected Kaká to spend his first year learning and developing while coming off the bench a little bit to get some game experience in Italy.

Besides, Milan already had a star midfielder in Manuel Rui Costa, a Portuguese legend. They also had Kaká's Seleção teammate Rivaldo, another midfielder. Kaká was willing to learn but also committed to contributing as much as he could to his new team.

"I knew that I had to adapt to European football," he later told England's *The Times*. "I am just one man, I knew it wasn't going to adapt to me. At the same time, I knew that if they signed me it was because I could provide something different." [1]

That something different was Kaká's blend of skillful style and physical strength. By now he was six feet, one inch, weighed about 180 pounds, and had fully grown into his body.

Former Brazilian national team coach Vanderlei Luxemburgo said, "Kaká has the technique of a Brazilian and the physical qualities of a European. He is the standard-bearer of the modern game." [2]

The question was: how long would he take to be able to fully show it?

Kaká's answer was: immediately. He wasted no time in making a big impression on his new coaches, teammates, and fans. Within his first week he scored his first goal in a preseason match against Genoa. In about a month he had earned a starting spot for the 2003–2004 season, pushing Rui Costa to the bench. When asked how he felt about it, Rui Costa answered, "He is simply extraordinary."[3]

Kaká usually played at the top of Milan's five-man midfield behind Ukrainian striker Andriy Shevchenko or Clarence Seedorf. Either way, it was a lethal combination. Kaká's vision of the field and understanding of where the game and its players were heading were exceptional. The Rossoneri wanted to get the ball to their midfielder, because he was able to move it up the field and deliver it at the feet of the goal-scoring specialists. But even while feeding passes to Milan's strikers, Kaká managed to score ten goals of his own in his first season.

Milan found itself in a heated three-way battle for first place in Serie A with Juventus and Roma. By December it appeared that the Rossoneri would be out of contention, but on January 6, Kaká's assist to Shevchenko enabled the winning goal over Roma that put Milan back on top. Kaká also contributed with a goal and assist against Inter Milan and an assist against Roma that gave Milan key victories. Milan won the Scudetto, the Serie A title, and Kaká was named the Player of the Year.

Naturally Milan's fans loved their new hero, which helped to make Kaká's transition to a new country easier. It wasn't too big a leap. The Italians are generally warm and expressive, much like Brazilians. And Milan has many similarities to São Paulo. Located in Northern Italy, it is the nation's largest city. Like São Paulo, it is a business and cultural center. It's also an international fashion capital. The stylish Kaká fit in well, as he was already a model and representative for the designer Giorgio Armani.

Kaká loved the delicious Italian food, as well. What was hard was being far away from his family and Caroline. While paparazzi looked for every opportunity to snap photos of the Brazilian celebrity, Kaká avoided them and the temptations of aggressive female fans by staying away from Milan's nightlife. He kept the same quiet lifestyle as he had back in Brazil, and didn't visit Milan's famous dance clubs.

Being 6,300 miles away from Caroline was difficult, but life for Kaká was off to an excellent start in Italy. AC Milan's president, Silvio Berlusconi, who also happens to be the Prime Minister of Italy, laughed and said, "It looks like the boy has a few good qualities, no?" [4] He also said that Kaká was far more valuable than every million they had paid to get him, calling the 8.5 million Euros "peanuts." [5]

Kaká took it all with humility. "He's a well-balanced, laid-back young man, who is not prone to either over-excitement or depression," coach Ancelotti said. "He is mentally very strong and already very mature beyond his years. I don't think there's much risk of him getting bigheaded. He is a great champion." [6]

San Siro Stadium

Home to both AC Milan and Internazionale, San Siro is a stadium icon in the world of soccer. It is officially named Stadio Giuseppe Meazza in honor of the player for Internazionale and AC Milan in the 1930s and 1940s. He was also a two-time World Cup winner. The stadium is more commonly called San Siro because of its location in the San Siro district of Western Milan. It underwent major renovations for the 1990 World Cup and currently seats almost 86,000. A museum located inside the stadium commemorates the history and achievements of both teams.

Learning the Hard Way

Opponents only thought they were ready for Kaká the next season. Opposing coaches studied the twenty-two year old's moves and tendencies and sent their best defenders to slow him down.

It made a difference, and Kaká was slowed down somewhat. Some media and experts criticized him for not being able to keep up the phenomenal pace of his first year, but Kaká knew he was young and still had plenty to learn.

"It has been more difficult than last year," Kaká said. "I am known in Italy now. The markers know me, and they are tough here." [1]

To adjust, Coach Ancelotti gave his playmaker more freedom to move wider on the wings. It gave him more room to escape from his markers, or it pulled his defenders wide, opening up more room in the middle for teammates to do their damage.

Kaká didn't score as many goals in 2005–2006, but he still finished with seven in thirty-six games. And he continued to become the leader of his team.

What some have called his greatest goal at Milan came in September at San Siro during an important EUFA Champions League match against Turkey's Fenerbahce. Kaká had scored the Rossoneri's first goal in the eighteenth minute on a low, twenty-four-yard drive just inside the post. But with the game tied 1–1 and less than five minutes to play, Kaká received the ball on the left wing. On a full-speed run, he shook off one defender and dodged another as he ducked toward the middle of the field. With a little open space, he blurred past another defender at the top of the box. It appeared they were standing still as the red and black of Kaká's number twenty-two jersey blew by. Now there was only the goalkeeper in his way. He took one more touch on the ball, then blasted a right-footed shot along the ground, below the goalie's lunge, and inside the near post. Goal!

The TV announcers compared the display to the legendary Argentine Diego Maradona. Such praise was becoming commonplace for the young Brazilian.

"Someone with Kaká's talent and qualities comes along only once every fifty years," said Carlos Alberto Parreira, Brazil's new national coach. "He is the future example for every player in the Brazil team."[2]

Even the great Pelé, widely considered the best to ever play the game, agreed. "In Brazil, we have very good players in all positions, but I think the outstanding talent at the moment is Kaká," Pele said. "He is very skillful and already one of the best players in the world." [3]

What dazzled most was Kaká's efficiency and elegance. His moves were not flashy and jittery-quick; instead, he attacked directly and glided by defenders, controlling the ball seemingly effortlessly at full speed. None of his motions was wasted. "He will always try to go vertically rather than horizontally," his coach Ancelotti said. "He will never take the extra, unnecessary touch." [4]

Perhaps what made him most dangerous of all was Kaká's work ethic. He always practiced and played hard, and he continued to listen to and learn from his coaches.

Kaká's favorite highlight came early in 2005. First he called Caroline's father from Milan and asked for permission to marry her. Then he took his sweetheart to Venice, the romantic Italian city where the streets are watery canals and boatmen sing as they row their gondolas.

At dinner Kaká offered her a beautiful ring and asked her to be his wife. She said yes, and the couple began planning to marry later that year.

Back on the field, a storybook soccer ending seemed to be lining up as well. All across Europe, the top teams from each league play games in a season-long tournament arranged by UEFA. The best of the best compete in the Champions League, first in round-robin play, then in best-of-two-game elimination rounds. The ultimate winner of a single final game is crowned the best team in Europe and is generally considered the best team in the world.

AC Milan had reached the finals of the Champions League and would face the English team Liverpool in the finals. The match couldn't have begun better for Milan. Captain Paolo Maldini volleyed in a shot within the first minute to give the Rosseneri an immediate lead. Liverpool came close on several scoring chances but Milan's keeper Dida came up with the saves. In the thirty-eighth minute, Kaká dribbled into Liverpool's side and passed the ball to Andriy Shevchenko, who passed to Hernán Crespo on the far post. Crespo buried a shot in the net: 2–0 Milan. Crespo struck again a minute before halftime, taking a pass from Kaká and chipping over Liverpool's goalie Jerzy Dudek.

With a three-goal lead at the half, Milan seemed to have the championship in hand, but Liverpool refused to surrender. The Reds shifted their lineup around and went on a desperate attack. Their efforts paid off quickly as captain Steven Gerrard headed in a cross from John Arne Riise nine minutes into the half. Liverpool was on the scoreboard. Vladimír Šmicer added another goal two minutes later, and the momentum was fully in Liverpool's favor.

Less than four minutes after that, Liverpool was awarded a penalty kick when Milan defender Gennaro Gattuso fouled Gerrard in the box. Xabi Alonso lined up the ball on the twelve-yard penalty stripe and faced off against goalkeeper Dida. The kick came low for the left post. Dida dove. Save! But the live ball rebounded out and Alonso pounced to send it into the net. Goal Liverpool! Tie game 3–3!

Milan fought back and nearly regained a lead at minute seventy. Dudek couldn't hold onto a low cross and Shevchenko sent a shot on goal, but the Reds defender Djimi Traore was standing on the goal line to clear the ball safely away. An incredibly close miss!

Kaká had the final chance to score before the end of the game, but he couldn't redirect Jaap Stam's header on goal. The game ended still tied. It would go to overtime.

Both teams had chances to score in extra time, and Milan came closest. Shevchenko sent a rocket on goal. Dudek made the save but the ball rebounded back to Milan's striker. Shevchenko fired again from point-blank six yards, but Dudek miraculously managed to deflect it over the bar. This game was going to a shootout.

Could Liverpool complete the unthinkable comeback? They now had an equal chance with penalty kicks. Milan's Serginho shot first and sent the ball sailing over the crossbar. Liverpool converted to take an edge. Andrea Pirlo was next for Milan, but Dudek dove to his right to make the save. Liverpool's Djibril Cisse scored on his attempt. Liverpool was up 2–0.

Milan converted its next kick, while Liverpool's next attempt was saved. Kaká stepped up next and scored to even the score at 2s. Liverpool's Smicer regained the edge for Liverpool though, and the Rossoneri's Shevchenko was up. A goal would make Liverpool's final attempt a must-make to win. A miss would mean immediate victory for the Reds.

Shevchenko struck the ball down the center, counting on Dudek to dive to one side or the other. Dudek lunged to his right, but with his trailing left hand was able to block the rising ball. Save! Liverpool claimed the victory in a truly amazing comeback. The Reds were the champions of Europe.

The Rossoneri and their fans were heartbroken. "We had six minutes of madness in which we threw away the position we had reached until then," Coach Ancelotti said after the match. "We are unhappy, but I think we lost in an honorable way." [5]

Kaká knew there was as much to learn in defeat as in victory—maybe more. It just wasn't nearly as much fun.

Radical Reputation

Kaká had grown famous across Europe—mostly for his exceptional play on the field. But his reputation was intriguing to many people. He was the total opposite of the soccer star stereotype. Big magazines, newspapers, and TV shows across the continent wanted to tell his story. Readers and viewers wanted to know what was behind the carefree smile and game heroics. And Kaká wanted to tell them about the God he loved.

He continued to wear his Jesus bracelet everywhere he went, and it was widely known that he had the phrase "God is faithful" stitched into his cleats. The young Brazilian took every opportunity to reflect his gratitude and praise to Jesus. After goals he pointed and looked to the sky offering credit to God. When he spoke with reporters he was honest and outspoken about his love and devotion to Christ. He became famous for giving generously to his church back home in Brazil, Renascer em Cristo, or Rebirth in Christ. With his huge salary, even a ten-percent tithe was a lot of money!

Kaká, right, and World Food Program's representative John Powell show a jersey after Kaká was named an ambassador against hunger by the U.N. World Food Program.

The playmaker also wanted to use his position of celebrity to serve others. "In Brazil we think we can help by using our image, the fact that we are very well known, to help others," Kaká said.[1] He found the perfect way to make a difference when the United Nations World Food Program invited him to become their youngest ever Ambassador Against Hunger.

Kaká had first encountered extreme poverty in Brazil when he was twelve and visited a *favela* with his mother. Brazilian *favelas* are slums that are often ruled by drug lords. It opened his eyes to the blessings and comforts of his own life as well as the intense suffering and needs of others.

He realized how widespread the problems of hunger and poverty were when he traveled with the Seleção to play in some of the poorer areas of Brazil. "You see people come and watch us train or play a match and then you know some of them are going home with no food on the plate," he said.[2]

Now he had an opportunity to raise awareness of the issues and try to bring help especially to children in poor countries. He worked with the U.N.'s Feed the World program and began visiting poor countries to try to bring hope and help find solutions. He also stayed connected to a ministry with his Brazilian church to help people fight drug abuse and avoid life on the streets.

The Rebirth in Christ church was the site of a happy occasion on December 23, 2005 — Kaká and Caroline's wedding day. It was a beautiful and joyful event. Seven hundred guests joined the couple to celebrate, including many of Kaká's Milan and Brazil teammates.

Kaká with his bride, Caroline Celico, during their wedding in Sao Paulo on December 23, 2005.

Longtime best friend Marcelo Saragosa stood beside Kaká as his best man, and Kaká even wrote a song to his bride for the occasion. Finally, after three years of dating and separation across the world, the couple were husband and wife.

Of course, the media in Brazil and Europe were interested in the festivities. The focus brought even more attention to Kaká and Caroline's faith, especially the fact that the couple had remained virgins until they were married. Sexual attitudes are generally loose in Brazil and Italy, and the fact was unbelievable that anyone—

especially a superstar like Kaká—had actually followed God's commandments to keep sex only for marriage.

The couple spoke honestly about it, admitting that avoiding temptation hadn't been easy. "If today our life is so beautiful, I think it's also because we have been able to wait," Kaká told the Italian edition of *Vanity Fair* magazine.[3]

Kaká and Caroline returned to Milan to make their new life together, continuing to serve God and represent him at every opportunity.

Soccer vs. Football

Why is the sport called soccer in North America while most of the world calls it football? Many people think the name soccer was made up by Americans, but it actually originated in England. In 1863 there were a number of different "football" games being played with slightly different rules. The rules were standardized by England's Football Association. The game became known as Association Football to distinguish it from Rugby Football and others. Association Football was soon shortened into *soccer*, a type of abbreviation take from "assoc." At the time, many of the upper class in England, including men who attended prestigious universities such as Oxford and Cambridge called it soccer.

When the game became established in America, it was still often called football. In fact, the organization that governs soccer still had "football" in its name until 1974. The organization was first known as the U.S. Football Association (1913–1944), then U.S. Soccer Football Association (1945–1973), and finally U.S. Soccer Federation (1974–current). Today the name soccer distinguishes the sport from American football, which has gained greater popularity in the United States.

The U.S. isn't the only country to use the term soccer. Canada, Ireland, and some in Australia, New Zealand, and South Africa use the term as well. But the majority of the world still prefers football.

Not-So-Magic in Germany

Kaká's on-field consolation after Milan's disappointments was Brazil's victorious Confederations Cup 2005. The prestigious tournament serves as a warm-up the year before each World Cup, and is limited to eight teams: the continental and regional champions of the world's soccer federations.

Brazil didn't look their best in the opening round, losing a close match to Mexico and tying Japan. But they did well enough to place second in the group and advance to the knockout rounds.

There the Canarinho edged mighty Germany 3–2 and thrashed their South American archrival Argentina 4–1 in the final. Kaká scored what turned out to be the winning goal in the sixteenth minute, and it has remained one of his favorites. "Every time you can score in a final, it's a completely different sensation from all the rest, and a fantastic feeling," he said later.[1]

The championship was yet another reason why the defending World Cup champions were widely seen as favorites heading into Germany 2006. The Seleção boasted the globe's biggest collection of superstars on one team. At its center was the "magic quartet." Ronaldo was on the verge of becoming the all-time World Cup leading scorer. Ronaldinho had won the FIFA World Player of the Year award, given to the best player in the world, the previous two years. Adriano was a dangerous striker from Kaká's cross-town rival club Inter Milan. And Kaká had developed into a world superstar since being the young rookie at the Cup four years earlier.

Brazil expected a championship from its Seleção once again. The only question was: could the collection of superstars work smoothly as a team?

The answer seemed to be *maybe*, or at least well enough. In the first opening round game, Brazil edged out Croatia in a close match. The Croatians pressed the Brazilian defense and goalkeeper Dida was heroic with several big saves. Just before halftime Emerson surged onto Croatia's half of the field and passed to Cafu, who slipped the ball inside to Kaká. Kaká switched the ball to his left and fired an unstoppable curling shot from the edge of the box. It was Brazil's brightest moment and enough to give them a win.

After the match, Kaká told the press, "A narrow victory is good to calm down fans who think that there will always be goals and a spectacle, because this thing that is said—that we are football's [Harlem] Globetrotters—is just not true." [2]

Brazil looked beatable, and they seemed to struggle to gel their attack. But the Seleção built some momentum with a 2–0 win over Australia, then finally seemed to find its form with a 4–1 victory over Japan. It was Ronaldo's breakout game of the Cup at last, and his two goals placed him in a tie on the World Cup all-time leading scorer list.

Brazil won its group and moved to the knockout round. Its foe in the quarterfinal match was Ghana, and the Africans' defense was no match for the Brazilian attack. Ronaldo netted again to become the all-time leading World Cup scorer with fifteen lifetime goals.

The World Cup was down to eight teams, and Brazil next faced France, an excellent team led by world stars Zinedine Zidane and Thierry Henry. From the start the French took control of the game, with playmaker Zidane setting the pace. But they could not break through Brazil's defense for any real scoring opportunities.

Kaká just missed a low cross from Ronaldo at the near post in the fifteenth minute, but most of the first half highlights came from Zindane's dazzling footwork. Ronaldinho tried to match the fancy French footwork early in the second half, but in the fifty-seventh minute, France struck. Zidane floated a free kick from the left side toward the far post. Henry was there to meet it with the side of his right foot, and he volleyed the ball into the goal. France took the lead 1–0.

With about thirty minutes left, Brazil changed its formation and shifted forward into its magic quartet. They pressed the attack, trying to find the net, and later made even more offensive substitutions. Ronaldo attempted several shots, but France packed its defense back and thwarted every attempt. Brazil could find no answer for Les Bleus, and the defending champions were sent home to Brazil.

As the Cup continued without the Brazilians, France went all the way to the finals to play Italy for the title. France seemed to be the superior team, but the score remained tied 1–1 after regulation and overtime. In the end, the Italians prevailed on penalty kicks.

Brazil's Coach Parreira took the blame for the Samba Kings' defeat, and Ronaldo and Ronaldinho apologized for their overall lackluster performances.

After the opening game, Brazil's 1970 World Cup-winning captain Carlos

Kaká celebrates after scoring against Fenerbahce during the Champions League Group E match in Milan, Italy. Kaká's trademark gesture of raising his hands to the sky shows his thanks to God for the talent he has been given.

Alberto told The Guardian newspaper, "Kaká was the only corner of the magic square that worked. The only way this tactical formation will be effective is if the players move around a lot. Ronaldinho tried to, but didn't manage. Ronaldo didn't do anything. Only Kaká managed to fit in." [3]

The same consensus seemed to hold true for most of the Cup, but it was little consolation for him. "The World Cup was a huge frustration because I had prepared really hard for it," Kaká said later. "But in the World Cup there is no formula, no recipe for success." [4]

Brazil's underachievement was blamed on the underwhelming performances of its biggest players. Of all its superstars in the magic quartet, it was only Kaká who had shone at all.

Both of his World Cups had defied original expectations. Both would serve as valuable learning experiences for different reasons.

World Cup Records at a Glance
(Prior to the start of the 2010 World Cup)

- Brazil is the only team to have played at every one of the 18 World Cups and has won a record five championships.

- Ronaldo of Brazil is the overall leading goal scorer, with 15 goals in three tournaments. He is followed by Germany's Gerd Müller with 14 goals, France's Just Fontaine with 13 goals, and Brazil's Pelé with 12 goals.

- Brazil and Germany have both played 92 matches, the most by any nation.

- Brazil has scored 201 total goals, the most in the history of the World Cup.

• So far, only Brazil's Mário Zagallo and West Germany's Franz Beckenbauer have won the World Cup as both player and head coach.

• Highest match attendance in a World Cup final tournament is 199,854, when Uruguay played Brazil on July 16, 1950 in Maracanã Stadium, Rio de Janeiro, Brazil.

Ronaldo

Ronaldo Luis Nazário de Lima, known as Ronaldo, is a favorite of Brazilian fans and considered to be their biggest soccer hero since Pelé. He rose to greatness in the 1990s and has played for a number of teams, including Internazionale, Real Madrid, AC Milan, and, of course, the Brazilian national team.

Ronaldo was named FIFA's World Player of the Year in 1996 and 1997. He was the youngest player to win the award as well as the first player to win the award two years in a row.

He has been part of Brazil's team in four World Cups:

• In 1994, at the age of 17, he was on the championship team but didn't play.

• In 1998 he gave a star performance but was criticized for Brazil's loss in the final.

• In 2002 he led Brazil to a World Cup championship and won the Golden Boot as the tournament's top scorer with eight goals.

• In 2006, despite accusations of being overweight and slow, he scored three goals for a lifetime total of 15 in World cup play—a new record.

After injuries in 2008 AC Milan didn't renew Ronaldo's contract. He returned to Brazil to play with Corinthians, and his fans still love him for playing with Brazilian flair.

Golden Year

2007 was Kaká's year. When Milan's striker Andriy Shevchenko departed for the English Premier League's Chelsea in the off-season, more responsibility fell to the twenty-four-year-old Kaká.

The team struggled a bit trying to find the right balance in its attack. Then Coach Ancelotti tried a new formation, with Kaká and Clarence Seedorf pushed forward as the main attackers.

At first, Kaká felt "a bit mesmerized," as he later described. His role had always been to create goal-scoring situations for the forwards. Now he was on the receiving end of most passes, expected to finish with the ball in the net.

"I have learned to have the mentality of a striker, because before I had a midfielder's mentality, and I still do, which is that of making the last pass," Kaká told

World Soccer later. "But forwards don't work that way. So now I have to finish the move myself." [1]

Like most things involving a soccer ball, Kaká picked up his new role quite well, though he claimed after the season that he still wasn't fully comfortable as a striker. That didn't keep him from scoring ten goals in Serie A, enough to make him the league leader.

But his most important strikes came during Champions League play. Milan advanced through UEFA group play as one of sixteen teams with a chance to claim the title. There, the Rossoneri first faced the Celtics from the Scottish Premier League. Champions League knockout rounds consist of teams playing each other twice for points, with each getting one home game. In the first match in Glasgow, Scotland, the two clubs battled to a scoreless tie. Back at the San Siro, things looked similar as the clock wound down. Neither team had been able to find the net.

Kaká came ever-so-close in the eighty-seventh minute. He chipped the ball from twenty yards and sent it sailing over the head of Celtic's goalkeeper Artur Boruc. Boruc was beat. It looked like the ball was going in—but it struck the crossbar and bounced clear.

The game went to overtime. Three minutes into the extra period Milan took the ball and launched a fast counterattack. Marek Jankulovski served the ball to Kaká at midfield. Kaká dribbled at a sprint past one defender, then outran two more toward the left post. As Boruc moved out to challenge and a Celtic defender tried to slide tackle, Kaká drove the ball between Boruc's legs for the goal that would prove to be the winner.

The Rossoneri moved through the Champions League, beating Celtic and Bayern Munich to set up a duel with mighty Manchester United. Manchester United is one of the most dominant teams in the English Premiere League and regularly one of the world's best. It is arguably the most famous team in the world, with an estimated 75 million fans who claim the Red Devils as their team.

What's intimidating is Old Trafford, United's home stadium, where 74,000 red-clad fans sing and chant for their team beneath banners that read *Manchester United The Religion*. That's where Milan would have to play first.

Besides being a clash between two of the world's top clubs, this pair of games was seen as a dual between two of the world's brightest young stars: Kaká and Cristiano Ronaldo. Ronaldo was United's Portuguese striker, who had an exceptional knack for finding the net. At the time he was on the verge of an astonishing forty-two goals. He played with a sensational flair, relying on quick dribbling and fancy footwork, and he had a reputation for being fiery and demanding. In many ways, he was the exact opposite of the smooth, straightforward Kaká.

United was heavily favored. The Red Devils were on the way to claiming the Premier League title back home in England. They had already won the prestigious FA Cup. Manchester also had beaten its last Champions League opponent, Roma, 7–1.

Against Milan, Ronaldo struck quickly for the English side, deflecting a corner kick into the back of the net only five minutes into the game. But then the game turned into Kaká's show. He found the net for Milan in the twenty-second minute to tie the score. With a beautiful dribble, he sped into the box past two United defenders and sent the ball inside the far post from an amazing angle.

United didn't let up its attack, though, and Milan's Dida was forced to make several diving saves. Kaká struck again in the thirty-seventh minute to give Milan a 2–1 lead at halftime. As he raced for the ball, so did two United defenders. Kaká managed to head the ball forward and sidestep around as they crashed into each other. With only the goalie left, Kaká shot a roller past his dive and inside the post.

Manchester United found the net next when Wayne Rooney shot past Dida from eighteen yards out. The game remained tied past the regulation ninety minutes before United launched a fast counterattack in the extra three minutes the ref added to make up for injury delays. Ryan Giggs sprinted down the right wing with the ball, passed it inside to Rooney near the corner of the box. Rooney smashed it inside the near post and into the net. It was a dramatic 3–2 win for Manchester United.

A week later the clubs squared off again, this time in San Siro. Kaká was determined to see a different result. Milan's Champions League's hopes depended on it.

Playing in the pouring rain, Kaká picked right back up with his scoring, giving Milan the lead just eleven minutes into the game. Clarence Seedorf headed a ball to the center, where the rushing Kaká charged and fired a low volley past the goalie, Edwin van der Sar. A few minutes later it was Seedorf's turn, using his chest to control a cross from the right side, then firing the ball past van der Sar. Later Alberto Gilardino made it 3–0 Milan when he sprinted into the penalty box alone and easily looped the ball into the goal in a one-on-one against van der Saar.

The game was all Milan—and all Kaká. His presence and playmaking was dominant throughout both games, and Manchester United had been unable to contain him. It was later called the greatest moment of his career, even more so than the coming Champions League final.

By splitting the games with a victory a piece, the determining factor between the two teams was the number of goals scored, and Milan had the edge 5–3. The Rossoneri were headed to the Champions League final.

For some time now, Kaká had been talked about as one of the best players in the world. Now the official awards began pouring in. Some of the most prestigious were the Ballon d'Or, or Golden Ball, given to the best player in the world, and the FIFPro World Player of the Year, voted on by more than fifty thousand soccer professionals around the world.

On December 17, 2007, Kaká walked onto the stage at the Zurich Opera House in Switzerland, where the Brazilian legend Pelé handed him the award for FIFA World Player of the Year, the most prestigious honor in soccer.

The honors brought the star player great satisfaction,

but he received them all with his normal humility and gratitude. In all his acceptance speeches and interviews, he genuinely thanked God, his family, his coaches, and teammates. Kaká recognized that he wouldn't be accepting all of the trophies without the help of great teammates.

Kaká, left, receives the trophy from soccer legend Pelé after being named FIFA World Player of the Year during the 17th Fifa World Player Gala in Zurich, Switzerland, Dec. 17, 2007.

With the sign of a great champion, Kaká knew that his awards didn't mean he was a perfect player. If anything, they fueled his desire to keep working hard. "My aim is to keep on listening and learning from others and to keep improving as a player and as a person," Kaká said after receiving the FIFPro trophy. "It is a privilege to be a professional footballer, and it is our duty to work hard to be the best we can be for our teammates, supporters, club, and country, and to earn the respect of fellow men." [2]

When asked later by *World Soccer* magazine if his Champions League victory had been the most important game of his life, Kaká answered, "No. The most important match in my life will always be the next one. You mustn't dwell too much on what has been achieved—or else you run the risk of losing motivation." [3]

His attitude all but ensured that the world had plenty yet to expect from Kaká, its most superior player.

Best Players in the World

Each year the FIFA World Player of the Year is given to the best male and female player, based on voting by coaches and captains of international teams.

Ballon d'Or

Since 1956 journalists have been voting to award the Golden Ball to the best player in the world. The Ballon d'Or started as an honor only for European players in a European club, but has come to be awarded to any player of any nationality.

Not about the Money

The breaking news rocked the soccer world. Manchester City was offering AC Milan more than 100 million British pounds, or $146 million, to Milan to let Kaká come play for their team in the English Premier League. And if the deal went through, Kaká would earn a half million dollars each *week*.

It was an astronomical sum even in the high-dollar world of soccer — or any pro sport, for that matter. The offer would more than double the previous record for the highest transfer fee: $65 million for Zinedine Zidane at Real Madrid in 2001. However, the Manchester City team had been purchased earlier in the year by Sheik Mansour bin Zayed al-Nahyan. He came from the royal family of Abu Dhabi, an oil-rich nation in the Middle East. He was willing to spare no expense to turn his team into a winner.

Kaká's initial response was that he loved playing at Milan and hoped to stay and eventually become captain of the team—but that the decision lay first with his club. In contract negotiations, a player's team owned the first right to decide whether to consider another team's offer. If Milan agreed, then Manchester City could talk directly with Kaká about making the move.

Milan loved its star player but was facing economic difficulties in the midst of the global economic recession. If they sold Kaká's contract, it would help them to balance their own budget and free up money for them to bring in other rising stars for less money. Manchester City's offer was too much for them to pass up, so Milan's executives agreed to the deal if Kaká said yes.

Milan's fans, on the other hand, were outraged. They protested in the streets outside Milan's headquarters and outside Kaká's house, waving banners and chanting for their star to stay with the Rossoneri. They loved their Brazilian star, and he loved them. One night he appeared at his window, waving down to the fans and holding a Milan jersey to his heart. Indeed, Kaká and Caroline had put down roots in their Italian city, and Kaká had even received Italian citizenship.

As negotiations continued with Kaká and his father, who was his professional agent, the soccer world speculated about what would happen. His former Brazilian national coach, Luiz Felipe Scolari, offered wise insight when he told The Associated Press, "I know Kaká very well. Money is not his problem." [1]

Kaká prayed about the decision and discussed it with his loved ones. In the end, Scolari was correct. Kaká announced he turn down the exorbitant amount of money to stay in Milan. "All the messages that I received said to choose with the heart, and I think in the end that has been the decision," Kaká said. "It is absolutely not about money." [2]

Milan rejoiced, and Kaká seemed relieved to return his attention to simply playing the game he loved. But the door had been opened to negotiate with Milan's star, and other clubs were quick to knock. Rumors swirled about another high bid from Chelsea, one of the Big Four teams from the English Premier League, but the attempted deal went nowhere.

Then came word that Real Madrid was in the mix, and in June 2009 it was official. Kaká was headed to play for the storied club in the Primera Division of the Liga de Futbol Profesional, better known as Spain's La Liga, another one of the strongest professional soccer leagues in the world. Although not as much as Manchester City's bid, 65 million Euros, or about $93 million, set a new record for the highest transfer fee ever.

Yet Kaká insisted that his decision had more to do with the possibilities of more championships on the field than his paycheck. "I knew I'd only leave Milan to play for Real," he told the BBC. "It's an important project for me to continue growing in my career. I'm not going to Real Madrid for money, as I had other offers. That's why I chose Madrid. They have historic players there already, such as Raul and Iker Casillas. It will be an important challenge for me. We're going to win many titles again." [3]

Winning championships was something Real Madrid was known for. The club has a record thirty-one La Liga titles and nine European Cups, also a record. The team was named the best club of the twentieth century after a detailed study of statistics by the International Federation of Football Statistics (IFFHS).

The Whites, as they are also called, had their last great era in 2000, when club leadership paid big dollars to bring in superstars, including Ronaldo, David Beckham, Zinedine Zidane, Luis Figo, Roberto Carlos, and Raul. It was the world's biggest collection of top talent in one place, and the group was known as the Galacticos. The team's emphasis was on overpowering other teams with its superpowered offense. The Galacticos era brought La Liga titles in 2001 and 2003, and a European Super Cup in 2002.

The 2008–2009 season saw rival Barcelona dominate La Liga, and Real Madrid brought back Florentino Perez, the club president who had assembled the Galacticos. He took the same strategy: the world's biggest dollars for the world's biggest players.

Kaká was the first blockbuster deal, but a few days later, 2008's World Player of the Year Cristiano Ronaldo was signed to Madrid. His deal broke the record set on Kaká, and 80 million pounds, or $129 million, made Cristiano Ronaldo the most expensive soccer player ever. The world's two best players were now teammates.

Soon the club added even more star power. Karim Benzema came from Olympique Lyonnais in France, and Xabi Alonso arrived from Liverpool to serve as the defensive anchor of the midfield. The total reached nine new players brought in, as well as coach Manuel Pelligrini.

Talk began right away of a new Galacticos II era led by Kaká and Cristiano Ronaldo. But neither liked the comparison. They preferred to establish their own new era, hopefully of success.

Kaká especially knew the importance of being more than a collection of star players. From the start he urged his teammates to put aside big egos and work hard.

"My experience in football tells me that talent is not enough. The Brazilian national team in 2006 had a lot of talent, but we were knocked out of the World Cup quarter-finals because we lacked many things which prevented us from succeeding," Kaká told *The Independent*. "Real Madrid have Cristiano and Benzema, and that's good because we are quality players, but we need to build a team and work very hard. Real Madrid won't become invincible just by signing us." [4]

On June 30, Kaká walked through the tunnel into Real Madrid's historic stadium, the Bernabeu, in his official Real Madrid uniform. There was no game to be played — yet. But there were 50,000 thousand fans in the stands cheering as their new player was introduced. It was a hero's welcome in Kaká's new playing home.

Santiago Bernabéu Stadium

Built in 1944, the stadium is named after the club's chairman at the time who had a vision for giving the fans of Real Madrid an amazing stadium to match their team. It currently holds 80,000 seated spectators, down from the 125,000 seated and standing spectators in the 1950s. It has hosted many exciting tournaments, including European Cup finals, European Nations' Cup, and the 1982 World Cup. While soccer is the main attraction here, the stadium occasionally hosts concerts as well.

Real Madrid

Full team name: Real Madrid Club de Fútbol
Nicknames: Many, including *Los Merengues* (which is a delicious cake of the rich), *Los Vikingos* (The Vikings), and *Los Blancos* (The Whites, because of their uniforms).
Home stadium: Santiago Bernabéu, Madrid, Spain.
League: La Liga
Founded: 1902
Main opponents: FC Barcelona and Atlético de Madrid.
Honors:

• Has won the most European Cups.

• Considered the richest club in the world based on revenue.

• Called "the most successful football club of the twentieth century" by FIFA.

• Named the best club of the 20th century after an in-depth study by the International Federation of Football History and Statistics (IFFHS).

Cristiano Ronaldo

Cristiano Ronaldo dos Santos Aveiro is a Portuguese player currently on the Real Madrid squad. Prior to coming to Spain, he played for Manchester United in England from the age of eighteen. Named the FIFA World Player of the Year in 2008, he is a forward with astonishing speed, dazzling ball control, and powerful shooting ability. Despite his amazing talent and the skill displayed in his performance leading up to big tournaments, some feel he hasn't lived up to expectations in international competition like the 2006 World Cup and Euro 2008. He was nicknamed Ronaldo after Ronald Reagan, his father's favorite actor.

The Spanish Liga

The top professional league in Spain is called The Primera División (First Division) of the Liga de Fútbol Profesional (Professional Football League). It is more commonly called La Liga. As in many other professional leagues, they adopt the relegation system where the three lowest ranked teams are relegated to a lower division, while the three highest-ranked teams from the lower division are promoted to La Liga. Real Madrid has dominated the competition since the 1950s and won their 19th title at the end of the 2008–09 season.

Champions Heading for the World Cup

This was not a place Brazil was used to being: losing at halftime—to the United States, no less. The Americans had played two brilliant games to reach this final of the 2009 Confederations Cup, but they were not one of the world's traditional soccer powers.

The Confederations Cup is an elite tournament held every four years in the year before the World Cup. The champions of each world soccer region, plus the current World Cup champion and the host country, make up the eight teams who play.

Brazil was the reigning champion of the South American Football Confederation, better known as CONMEBOL. It was also the defending Confederations Cup champion. The United States had won the Confederation of North, Central American, and Caribbean Association Football (CONCACAF).

Brazil's first game had been against a tenacious Egypt. The Seleção jumped to a 3–1 lead by halftime, but the Pharoahs fought back to tie. Egypt brought it even again ten minutes into the second half. The match seemed destined for a tie. But when an Egyptian player touched the ball with his hands, Brazil was awarded a penalty kick. Kaká got the ball into the goal, giving Brazil a narrow victory.

The Canarinho rolled through its next two opening round games, dismantling the United States 3–0 and Italy 3–0. It seemed the Brazilians were back to their unbeatable selves.

The host nation, South Africa, played tougher than expected in the semifinal match, and it took a late curling free kick in the final two minutes to find the net and seal another victory for the Brazilians.

On the other side of the bracket, the United States faced off against Spain, the number one team in the world. Everyone expected a Brazil-Spain showdown in the final.

The Americans had struggled early in the tournament, losing 1–3 to Italy and 0–3 to Brazil. Going into their last first-round game against Egypt, the Yanks had an extremely slim chance to claim second place in its group and enable them to advance. If the U.S. could beat Egypt by three *and* if Italy lost to Brazil by three, then the U.S. could advance on a mathematical tie-breaker. It was a long shot—but it was a shot.

The Americans knew anything can happen in international soccer—and it did. The United States won

3–0. Brazil beat Italy 3–0. Amazingly, the U.S. moved on. The final was set for a Brazil versus United States rematch. Could the Americans find yet another miracle?

Riding their never-say-day euphoria from the Spain victory, the Americans came out hard and strong and netted first only ten minutes into the game. Brazil seemed stunned and flat, and the Americans dominated the first half, taking a 2–0 lead into the locker room at halftime. The Brazilians remained optimistic. "We can do it," they told each other. "We can turn the match around. Let's go."

The second half was a completely different story. It only took one minute in the second half for Luis Fabiano to score for Brazil. Kaká took control and began to orchestrate a Brazilian attack that sent the Americans reeling. The shots began to flow for the Seleção. Tim Howard, the American goalie, made spectacular saves, but the momentum was flowing green and gold.

In the sixtieth minute, Kaká headed a ball off the underside of the crossbar before Howard grabbed it. The Brazilians called for a goal. The referee said to play on. TV replays showed that the ball had indeed crossed the goal line, but there are no instant replays in soccer. The U.S. held its narrow lead, even when Luis Fabiano's pointblank blast was saved by Howard.

Fifteen minutes from the end of regulation play, Kaká carried the ball down the left wing, eluded defender Jonathan Spector, and crossed to Elano. The shot struck the crossbar, bounced back in front of the goal, and was headed in by Luis Fabiano. Tie game.

Both teams pushed hard to find a winning goal. Five minutes before the end of regulation, Brazil was awarded a corner kick. Elano struck a beautiful cross that curved away from the goal to the back corner of the penalty box. Lucio leaped over Clint Dempsey and headed a rocket between the post and a lunging Howard. Brazil had battled back to win 3–2.

As the Brazilians danced and celebrated their victory, some of the Americans wept openly. Kaká wore his trademark "I belong to Jesus" T-shirt alongside Lucio in his own "I love Jesus." The comeback victory showed the resilience and heart of the skilled Brazilian squad.

Kaká was given the Golden Ball award in the ceremony following the game. Teammate Luis Fabiano claimed the Golden Shoe for overall leading scorer. And the entire Brazilian team received the Fair Play Award for their graceful play and enthusiastic sportsmanship.

As usual, Kaká deflected praise to his teammates. "The most important thing, as I've always said, is to win as a unit. All of that happened and Brazil was the champion," he said following the final match. "If it hadn't been for the team I wouldn't have been the best player or the man of the match." [1]

The victory helped to secure Brazil as a favorite heading into the 2010 World Cup in South Africa. It also gave Brazilian fans confidence in their Seleção.

After its disappointing 2006 World Cup, Dunga took over as coach and shook up the squad. He benched all the superstars, including Ronaldo, Ronaldinho, and even Kaká, making it clear that everyone must earn their spot based on hard work and solid performance. Dunga had been the captain of the 1994 World Cup champions team, and as a player was known as a tough defender. As a coach he emphasized disciplined, tactical soccer, and many Brazilians criticized and complained, claiming that their Seleção was no longer playing the improvised but beautiful game Brazil had always been known for.

Of course, Kaká emerged as just the type of player to lead the re-made Brazilians with his mix of fundamental skills, efficient passing, and killer scoring ability. The team struggled with some of its early international results but built solid momentum in 2009 by winning the Confederations Cup and securing qualification for the World Cup. And the more they won, the more the demanding nation of Brazil began to believe in the new vision of its team. Still, they will expect nothing less than a championship in South Africa come summer 2010.

Kaká and his teammates are committed to nothing less, and Kaká has said it's his number one goal for 2010. But he and his teammates know the road is long to reach that destination.

Dunga

Carlos Caetano Bledorn Verri, better known as Dunga, is a former Brazilian defensive midfielder known for a tough, no-nonsense playing style — different than the artistic, beautiful game Brazilians love. He anchored the team defense for its 1994 World Cup victory.

As a coach he has emphasized hard teamwork over individual stardom. Many Brazilians have criticized him for it, claiming he is trying to turn the Seleção into a European-style team. Love him or hate him, Brazilians will be watching to see if Dunga's determination can bring World Cup victory again.

World Cup 2010

The nineteenth World Cup kicks off June 11, 2010, in South Africa. Here are the thirty-two teams that have earned their way to the world's grandest championship.

Group A

- South Africa
- Mexico
- Uruguay
- France

Group B

- Argentina
- Nigeria
- Korea Republic
- Greece

Group C

- England
- USA
- Algeria
- Slovenia

Group D

· Germany
· Australia
· Serbia
· Ghana

Group E

· Netherlands
· Denmark
· Japan
· Cameroon

Group F

· Italy
· Paraguay
· New Zealand
· Slovakia

Group G

· Brazil
· Korea DPR
· Côte d'Ivoire
· Portugal

Group H

· Spain
· Switzerland
· Honduras
· Chile

South Africa: Host of the World Cup 2010

- The Republic of South Africa is located on the southern tip of the continent.

- The government is a democracy, with the president as the head of state.

- The country is rich with natural beauty: lakes, mountains, hills, coast, and plains.

- It is known as the Rainbow Nation. This refers to the richness of the people of South Africa — diverse cultures, histories, and languages. While English is most commonly used in official business, there are eleven officially recognized languages.

- Football is sometimes called soccer and colloquially referred to as *diski*.

- South Africa's history was marked by violent racist political and economic policy that discriminated against non-whites. This system of government was called Apartheid.

- South Africa was banned from international soccer competition for nearly three decades because of Apartheid.

- In the seventeen years since being allowed to play again, South Africa has shown its strength and talent in international soccer.

Toward the Goal

In many ways, Kaká is the prime example of the new global soccer star. Many Latin Americans, especially Brazilians, have reached the top levels of European soccer, but from the start Kaká has been a rare combination of the best of both worlds: the elegant creativity of South America mixed with the tactical strategy of Europe. Kaká's game is both beautiful and smart. His incredible ball-controlling skills are used more often to make an amazing assist for a teammate's goal, but his own dangerous shooting and scoring keeps opposing goalkeepers on edge.

Just before their Confederations Cup showdown, the best American player Landon Donovan described Kaká like this, "When they are comfortable in possession, he does a good job of just moving the ball and keeping things going. And then when he sees an opportunity with some space to go, he takes off and he's gone. He makes the right pass, he's good in front of the goal. Physically, he's so gifted. You forget that he's so big, he's strong, and how fast he is. In a lot of ways, he's the ideal soccer player." [1]

"He's one of the two best players in the world," American and English Premier League goalkeeper Tim Howard added. "He's amazing because most of what he does is without flair. I think Cristiano Ronaldo is the other best player in the world, but he does it with flair. With Kaká, everything seems to be so simple for him, which is frustrating." [2]

Yet with all of the praise, awards, and accomplishments Kaká has received, it's his character and personal life that set him apart as a true champion. The twenty-eight-year-old has consistently kept his priorities in order: faith, family, then football.

On the verge of winning his Champions League title with Milan, he said, "The best goal of my life would be to become a father and hold my first child in my arms." [3] A little over a year later, Caroline gave birth to their son, Luca, on June 10, 2008. When Kaká is not on the field, his favorite activity is relaxing with his family.

He remains outspoken about his love for Jesus and continues to back up his words. On the field he plays fair and remains positive, and off the field he still works with the United Nations to bring food and opportunity to children in the world's poorest areas. As he has thought about what he will do when he eventually retires from professional soccer, Kaká has expressed the desire to study theology.

"I want to be an evangelical pastor," he told *GQ Italy*.

"It is not easy to apply things written thousands of years ago. But that is the job of a good shepherd." [4]

In late 2008 he got some practice when Kaká spoke during the Billy Graham Evangelistic Association event, My Hope Brazil, that was televised across the nation. "I have been named the best soccer player in the world," he said. "This for me was a great honor. But the greatest honor is serving Jesus Christ, because he gives me hope." [5]

Caring more about serving God than being the best soccer player has helped Kaká remain humble. He recognizes the true source of his talent. "Everyone receives a gift from God, and mine is football," he said. [6]

He also recognizes that it takes a complete team to win at soccer. He takes every opportunity to point out that he is no more important than the other ten players on the field with him, whether that is with the talented Real Madrid club or Brazilian Seleção.

But that doesn't mean he doesn't take his game seriously. He remains committed to working hard to always trying to improve. Kaká maintains a sharp competitive drive even though he has already accomplished so much. After his Italian Scudetto and World Player of the Year awards in 2007, he said, "My goal now is to win everything twice." [7]

He is poised to do that. Another World Cup title is a real possibility for the Brazilians in South Africa during summer 2010. And the star-studded group at Real Madrid certainly are within striking range of multiple La Liga and Champions League titles.

Goals on the field have helped to secure Kaká's legacy. But setting goals off the field have always been a motivating force. He quickly achieved the original ten goals he made while healing from his life-threatening neck injury. Then he continued to set—and accomplish—new goals, laying out clear plans of where he wanted to go and working daily to get there.

"I started kicking the ball just for fun," Kaká told *The Telegraph*. "But little by little I fell in love with the game and thought about the possibility of becoming a professional player. In the end I have reached places I had never dreamed of getting to."[8]

One could say Kaká's goals have paved that incredibly successful road he has traveled. There is no doubt that road will continue to carry Kaká to many more soccer feats. And along the way, the watching world will continue to gain motivation and inspiration from the beaming Brazilian always pressing forward, elegantly executing the dance between man and ball, embracing gracefully his role as the world's new ambassador of the beautiful game and giving credit where it is ultimately due.

"More than anything else, I need Jesus in my life," Kaká said. "I am successful in my financial life and in my professional life, but all this has come from God and is a gift of grace from him for my life. I will never stop following him."[9]

And with that, he presses on—always toward the goal.

Marucia Kintschev/AFP/Getty Images

Kaká with his wife, Caroline, and son, Luca, in Sao Paulo, Brazil, on June 10, 2008.

Acknowledgments

Special thanks to the following people who helped to make this book possible. Your insights, perspectives, assistance, and contributions are deeply appreciated.

Marcelo Saragosa, Eduard Cauich, Amy Hanson, Brett Honeycutt, Alex Marestaing, Lasal Miller, Lou Smith, Gary Booker, David McCasland, David Shrift, Rebecca Levine, Annette Bourland, Kathleen Kerr, Kris Nelson, and Kim Tanner.

Endnotes

Chapter 4

1. Athletes in Action interview for upcoming video in 2010, *The Prize: Chasing a Dream*.

2. Rob Draper, "Scolari and Kaká, a match made in heaven; Will the superstar who prefers Bible class to nightclubs bring sexy football to Chelsea?" *Mail on Sunday* (London), July 20, 2008, FB Edition.

3. "City would be getting the best," *Irish Times*, January 17, 2009.

4. "Q&A: Kaká," *FourFourTwo.com* interview, *http://fourfourtwo.com/interviews/qanda/39/article.aspx*.

5. Athletes in Action interview.

Chapter 5

1. "Player to Watch: Kaká is the new 'White Pelé'" *FIFA.com*, May 26, 2004, *http://www.fifa.com/worldcup/archive/germany2006/news/newsid=18215.html*.

2. *FourFourTwo.com* interview with Kaká.

3. Sam Wallace, "How Milan's prized asset became a class apart; Kaká's story is not the usual Brazilian tale of rags to riches," *Independent* (London), January 15, 2009, Second Edition.

4. Athletes in Action interview for upcoming video in 2010, *The Prize: Chasing a Dream*.

Chapter 6

1. "São Paulo 2x1 Botafogo – Final do Rio-SP 2001," *YouTube*

video of Rio-Sao Paulo Tournament goals, translated by Amy Hanson.

Chapter 7

1. Luciana Franca, "Kaká turns beast," *Istoe Gente* 168, (October 21, 2002), translated by Amy Hanson.

2. Franca, "Kaká turns beast."

3. "Kaká," *Veja Cronologia, http://veja.abril.com.br/cronologia/kaka/index.html.*

4. *FourFourTwo.com* interview with Kaká.

Chapter 8

1. *The Prize: Quest for the Ultimate Goal,* DVD, by Athletes in Action and The Film Foundry (2006).

2. *The Prize: Quest for the Ultimate Goal,* Athletes in Action.

3. Franca, "Kaká turns beast."

Chapter 9

1. *The Prize: Quest for the Ultimate Goal,* Athletes in Action.

2. "Brazil crowned world champions," *BBC Sport,* June 30, 2002, *http://news.bbc.co.uk/sport3/worldcup2002/hi/matches_wallchart/germany_v_brazil/default.stm.*

3. Duncan Castles, "Meet Brazil's Rooney... without the swearing and the sex scandals," *Daily Mail* (London), February 21, 2005.

Chapter 11

1. Gabriele Marcotti, "Milan's Kaka is a Brazilian superstar with vision but no vices," *Times Online,* January 15, 2009, *http://*

www.timesonline.co.uk/tol/sport/football/premier_league/manchester_city/article5518949.ece.

2. "Player to Watch: Kaká is the new 'White Pelé,'" FIFA.com, May 26, 2004, *http://www.fifa.com/worldcup/archive/germany2006/news/newsid=18215.html.*

3. Andy Mitten in Barcelona, "The golden boy of a golden team," *Independent* (London), Sunday, June 4, 2006, *http://www.independent.co.uk/sport/football/internationals/the-golden-boy-of-a-golden-team–481010.html.*

4. "Kaká," *Veja Cronologia.*

5. Ned Temko, "Kaká: A footballer of faith and fable," *Observer* (England), January 18, 2009, *http://www.guardian.co.uk/football/2009/jan/18/kaka-profile.*

6. "Player to Watch: Kaká is the new 'White Pele.'"

Chapter 12

1. "The Red Diff Interview," *http://www.ricardo-kaka.com/interview_02.php.*

2. Castles, "Kaká."

3. "Player to Watch: Kaká is the new 'White Pele.'"

4. Temko, "Kaká: A footballer of faith and fable."

5. "Ancelotti shattered after defeat," *BBC Sport,* May 25, 2005, *http://news.bbc.co.uk/sport2/hi/football/europe/4574893.stm.*

Chapter 13

1. "The Red Diff Interview."

2. "The Red Diff Interview."

3. Sara Faillaci, "Kaká and the sex of angels," *Vanity Fair* 23 (June 14, 2007).

Chapter 14

1. Athletes in Action interview for upcoming video in 2010, *The Prize: Chasing a Dream.*

2. Alex Bellos, "How privileged Kaká made most of luck to become Brazil's master of magic: Middle-class midfielder is tipped to be champions 'best performer on and off pitch," *Guardian* (England), June 17, 2006, *http://www.guardian.co.uk/football/2006/jun/17/worldcup2006.sport7?showAllComments=true.*

3. Bellos, "How privileged Kaká made most of luck to become Brazil's master of magic."

4. "Kaka Profile," *AskMen.com.*

Chapter 15

1. Andrea de Pauli, " 'We have neared perfection' Kaká reflects on Milan's Champions League triumph," *Sports Illustrated,* July 30, 2007.

2. "Kaká voted FIFPro World Player of the Year," FIFPro Official Award website, May 10, 2007, *http://worldx1.fifpro.org/index.php?mod=one&id=16922.*

3. de Pauli, " 'We have neared perfection.' "

Chapter 16

1. "City would be getting the best," *Irish Times.*

2. "Man City move for Kaká collapses," *BBC Sport,* January 20, 2009, *http://news.bbc.co.uk/sport2/hi/football/teams/m/man_city/7838966.stm.*

3. "Kaká completes Real Madrid switch," June 9, 2009, *http://news.bbc.co.uk/sport2/hi/football/europe/8082147.stm.*

4. "Kaká: Real Madrid players must work hard," *Independent*

(London), July 14, 2009, *http://www.independent.co.uk/sport/football/european/Kaká-real-madrid-players-must-work-hard-1745307.html*.

Chapter 17

1. "Dunga reveals unwavering belief," *FIFA.com*, June 29, 2009, *http://www.fifa.com/confederationscup/news/newsid=1077848.html#dunga+reveals+unwavering+belief.*

Chapter 18

1. Jere Longman, "Kaká Gives Brazil a Touch of Class in Confederations Cup," *New York Times,* June 21, 2009.

2. Longman, "Kaka Gives Brazil a Touch of Class in Confederations Cup."

3. Mark Ryan, "Sunday History beckons for the world's greatest footballer," *Mail on Sunday* (London), May 20, 2007.

4. Simone Stenti, "K factor," *GQ Italy* (December 2007).

5. "Faith in the Field," *Living Light News Online, http://www.livinglightnews.org/story2_07.09.htm* (August 28, 2009).

6. Julio Maldonado, "Kaká: The Sao Paulo years (II)," *Realmadrid.com,* June 12, 2009, *http://www.realmadrid.com/cs/Satellite/en/1202773849119/noticia/Noticia/Kaká:_The_Sao_Paulo_years_(II).htm.*

7. "Quero ganhar tudo duas vezes," *Veja.com,* December 19, 2007, *http://veja.abril.com.br/191207/p_128.shtml,* translated by Amy Hanson.

8. Ben Lyttleton, "Kaká beats Cristiano Ronaldo to Ballon d'Or," *Telegraph.co.uk,* November 25, 2007, *http://www.telegraph.co.uk/sport/football/european/2326589/Kaká-beats-Cristiano-Ronaldo-to-Ballon-dOr.html.*

9. Transcript, *The Prize: Chasing the Dream.*

We want to hear from you. Please send your comments about this book to us in care of zreview@zondervan.com. Thank you.